KT-140-456

DELICIOUS
HOME COOKING

DELICIOUS
HOME COOKING

Caroline Conran

Photography by Peter Williams

CONRAN OCTOPUS

For my family

EDITOR: Beverly LeBlanc
EDITORIAL ASSISTANT: Clare Blackwell
ART DIRECTOR: Mary Evans
DESIGNERS: Sue Storey, Peter Butler
ILLUSTRATOR: Lynne Robinson
PICTURE RESEARCHER: Abigail Ahern
FOOD STYLIST: Jane Suthering
PROP STYLIST: Róisín Neild
PRODUCTION CONTROLLER: Mano Mylvaganam

First published in 1992 by Conran Octopus Limited
37 Shelton Street, London WC2H 9HN
Most of these recipes have been previously published in
British Cooking and *Good Home Cooking*.

First UK trade edition
published in 1993 by
Conran Octopus Limited

This paperback edition
published in 1995 by
Conran Octopus Limited

Text © Caroline Conran 1992
Photography copyright © Peter Williams 1992
Design and layout copyright © Conran Octopus 1992

All rights reserved. No part of this book may be reproduced,
stored in a retrieval system or transmitted in any form or by
any means, electronic, electrostatic, magnetic tape, mechanical,
photocopying, recording or otherwise, without the prior
permission in writing of the publisher.

The right of Caroline Conran to be identified as Author of this
Work has been asserted by her in accordance with the Copyright,
Design and Patents Act 1988.

British Library Cataloguing in Publication Data.
A catalogue record for this book is available from
the British Library.

ISBN 1 85029 671 5

Typeset by Servis Filmsetting Limited
Printed and bound in Singapore

Please note the following:

Eggs used are size 3 (60–64 g) unless otherwise specified. The
government recommends that eggs not be consumed raw, and people
most at risk, such as children, old people, invalids and pregnant
women, should not eat them lightly cooked. This book includes
recipes with raw and lightly cooked eggs, which should not be eaten
by the above categories. These recipes are marked by an * in the text.
Once prepared, these dishes should be kept refrigerated and used
promptly.

Spoon measurements are level unless otherwise stated.

Metric and imperial measures are both given. Use one or the
other as the two are not interchangeable.

CONTENTS

INTRODUCTION

*L*ike many people who love food, my first ideas about it came from home – from intense experiences such as the unopposed temptation to eat some of the cold steak and kidney pie sitting on the slate in the larder ready for the next day's lunch, or the shrimps and winkles we boiled on the beach in billycans and devoured with cups of tea and bread and butter. Much of my childhood was spent near the sea in East Anglia; walking on the marsh, we stepped on samphire with every tread, and sucked the stalks raw. At the Swan Hotel in Southwold, we ate crab sandwiches and fought with the elderly residents to get the largest slices of Dundee cake from the tea trolley.

In fact, it was not until I left school that I tasted anything more 'foreign' than macaroni cheese or lamb curry, made from the leftovers of a roast leg of lamb with raisins and apples. Nor had I been to a restaurant, apart from the ones we tried on seaside outings. The food we had at home was plain and simple British food – the most wonderful roasts, pies and puddings, vegetables from the garden, mushrooms we gathered, our own fruit, home-made jams and marmalade, home-made cakes, home-made everything. We ate incredibly well.

So for me, the picture that the words 'delicious home cooking' conjure up is a timeless one – a group of people sitting round a table eating together in warm companionship. British food fits this picture perfectly, since it has evolved to be completely compatible with home life. Home-cooking means just that; this is the sort of food that brings an element of continuity and stability into a home. It is now known that the families that thrive are those that spend enough time together to talk things through and to air their experiences and grievances. The best and easiest way of achieving this is to sit round a table together as often as possible and share a meal. Most British people have long memories for the food of their childhood and no matter how sophisticated and wide-ranging people's taste may become as adults, they always respond to the good-tempered dishes that were served when they were young.

The majority of dishes in the British repertoire can be shared with children, are rarely very rich and many can be kept waiting without spoiling – in fact, the long-cooked fish pie or apple crumble with its crisp caramelized edge, can be even better than the just-cooked one. And after the first few times most of our dishes are simplicity itself to make; precise weights and measures are no longer necessary. After a while, most home cooks get an instinctive feeling for what is needed as they go along, and eventually the dish becomes their own, particular to their table.

The great rules to follow when you are cooking British dishes (almost any dish, in fact) are to be relaxed and not to skimp; be generous with the ingredients. For instance, a lump of butter on new potatoes and on plain vegetables will achieve total transformation of the humble and boring. It also brings out the depth of flavour in special ingredients such as asparagus. Be generous with your attention as well – even when something is quietly simmering in the oven, have a look every now and then to see if it needs skimming, check if the oven is too hot or if it is cooking too fast, or if the pot needs more liquid. Taste all the time. This is especially important with simple food; it is surprising, for example, how mashed potatoes need to be seasoned before and again after they are mashed, even if there was salt in the cooking water.

Because of the exceptionally friendly quality of British food, it offers one of the most stress-free ways of entertaining. The cook can be relaxed because the ground is familiar and everything comes naturally; guests can relax because the food is not pretentious, pompous or over-elaborate. And now it need not be heavy either, since British cooking has responded to the new passion for lightness and healthiness in food. The ingredients available today are as fresh as they have ever been – meat is less fatty, fish is fresher and vegetables are smaller and younger; there are light oils such as sunflower which make food cooked in lard or even in beef dripping, as it always

used to be, seem like a bad dream. And although, perhaps to avoid getting too moral, we still love chocolate desserts and traditional favourites, such as steak and kidney or treacle puddings, today the suet crust no longer has to be as thick as it traditionally was; it takes less to fill us up. We also cook with less flour now, so soups and sauces are light instead of stodgy. The word 'stodge' was at one time a descriptive epithet for British food, but not any longer. Another joke was our over-cooked vegetables, but now we cook them more rapidly and for shorter times to preserve their textures, colours and, in many cases, flavours.

The range of British dishes is finely tuned to the weather and has always been in harmony with the seasons and the produce that flourishes in our climate. British ingredients are good, and the fact that they still vary with time of year in spite of the influx of produce from all over the world, means we can positively look forward to the changing seasons. To autumn with its cornucopia of oysters, game, wild mushrooms, chestnuts and blackberries, and to winter with the crusty pies, crisp roasts, bronzed hot-pies and comforting puddings, all restorative food on a cold or miserable day. Spring brings fresh fish and wonderful asparagus and rhubarb, and probably the most delicious lamb in the world, followed in early summer by wild salmon and green peas and broad beans, new potatoes, strawberries and raspberries.

A revolution in food farming methods has brought about massive changes in recent years. As a result, certain ingredients, such as salmon and pheasant, are now much cheaper than they once were, as is cream. Different varieties of oysters have brought these back within reach again,

SEAFOOD COCKTAIL (PAGE 14)

and chickens are now everyday food, rather than the rare treat they used to be – and guinea fowl, duck, farmed pigeons and quails are now to be found more easily.

Personally, as far as vegetables, fruit and game are concerned, I try to cook more or less within the range of what is naturally in season, and to find as wide a variety of different shellfish, fish, poultry and meat as I can. If I am cooking British food, I leave out aubergines and green peppers, and go rather easy on the garlic and olive oil, keeping such things for Mediterranean dishes. I find that I can have, say, an Italian dish, such as grilled squid, or some taramasalata, or a slice of pâté before an English roast, but a meal made up entirely of British dishes can have a harmony of its own, which is the most satisfying of all.

STARTERS AND SOUPS

A starter should be spring-like, with fresh colours and light textures, the harbinger of more abundant things to follow. It should encourage appetite rather than dull it. When they are available, simple ingredients such as fresh asparagus, smoked salmon or freshly picked mushrooms cooked in cream make the easiest and best way to start a meal.

Although, of course, there are particular soup recipes that call for specific ingredients, the real joy of making soup is that you can make it with absolutely anything. So if you see lopsided asparagus in the shops at a bearable price, or cheap tomatoes, or if you have a glut of Swiss chard in the garden, or beetroot tops or too many of almost any vegetable, or if the broad beans you bought are not as young as you hoped, each one of these can be made into wonderful soups.

MUSSEL CHOWDER (PAGE 31)

EGG MOUSSE

This is the essential and original recipe for an egg mousse. You can add, with the herbs, cooked prawns or langoustines dusted with cayenne pepper, or cooked shelled mussels, arranged on the bottom of the dish, on top of the boiled eggs. Plain or elaborate, it is a delicate summer dish.

SERVES 8

6 eggs
1 bunch fresh tarragon
600 ml (1 pint) chicken consommé
(bought or home-made)

4 leaves or 15 g ($\frac{1}{2}$ oz) powdered gelatine (enough to set 600 ml/1 pint)
1 bunch fresh chives
1 tablespoon dry sherry
good double shake Tabasco sauce
150 ml ($\frac{1}{4}$ pint) single cream
150 ml ($\frac{1}{4}$ pint) double cream
salt and freshly ground black pepper
a few leaves of flat parsley or dill

*H*ard-boil the eggs for 10 minutes, then run them under cold water to cool; set aside. Strip the tarragon leaves from their stalks and put the stalks into 150 ml ($\frac{1}{4}$ pint) consommé; heat it in a small pan, infuse for 5 minutes to absorb

INDIVIDUAL EGG MOUSSES

the tarragon flavour and then use it to dissolve the gelatine. Strain the liquid, then combine it with the remaining consommé. Set aside a scant 150 ml ($\frac{1}{4}$ pint).

Chop the tarragon leaves and chives quite finely and stir them into the remaining 450 ml ($\frac{3}{4}$ pint) consommé. Allow it to cool but not quite set, then stir in the sherry and Tabasco.

Put the 2 creams into a bowl and whip until thick but not very stiff, then stir into the tarragon- and chive-flavoured consommé. Taste the mixture for seasoning and adjust if necessary.

Slice the hard-boiled eggs. Keep 8 slices for decoration and put the rest into the bottom of 8 ramekins or a 1.5 litre (2½ pint) soufflé dish.

Pour on the mousse mixture and chill in the refrigerator until firm. Arrange 1 slice of egg in the middle of each ramekin with a flat parsley leaf or dill sprig on top – dip these in the remaining consommé to keep them in place. Then chill again and lastly pour over the 150 ml (¼ pint) reserved consommé, which should be cool but still liquid. Chill. Serve with Granary toast and butter and a bottle of chilled Chablis.

BAKED EGGS*

Eat these delicious creamy eggs plain as a breakfast dish, or with toast as a first course. In the same way as there are endless omelettes, there are many ways to make baked eggs. They are particularly good with prawns, flaked smoked haddock or mushrooms that have been cooked in butter. You can also try them with cooked chicken livers or little strips of ham dusted with Parmesan cheese. Chives are also very good with either of these variations.

SERVES 2 OR 4

1 tablespoon salted butter
4 free-range eggs (*see page 4 for advice on eggs)
4 tablespoons double cream
cayenne pepper

*P*reheat the oven to 350°F (180°C, Gas 4). Butter 4 small cocottes or ramekins generously.

Break an egg into each and pour 1 tablespoon cream over each egg. Dust with cayenne pepper and bake for 8–10 minutes. Eat these eggs straight from the cocottes or ramekins.

Let each person put their own salt on; if you put salt on before cooking it makes spots on the eggs. If using a filling, put it in the bottom of the cocotte or ramekin when you add the butter, then break the egg on top.

ANOTHER SORT OF BAKED EGGS

Instead of putting cream on top, put a nut of butter underneath each egg. It will come up the sides of the egg making it slightly 'fried' round the edges, delicious to serve for breakfast.

FARMHOUSE-FRESH EGGS FOR SALE IN SUSSEX.

SPECIALITY EGGS
SEE PAGE 4 FOR ADVICE ON EGGS.

HENS' EGGS ARE A STAPLE OF MOST KITCHENS BUT OTHER BIRDS' EGGS ARE JUST AS VERSATILE, OFTEN ADDING A UNIQUE FLAVOUR OR EXTRA RICHNESS.

TRY THESE:

DUCK EGGS RICH-FLAVOURED EGGS WITH TRANSLUCENT, WAXY IVORY SHELLS THE SIZE OF LARGE HENS' EGGS. COUNTRY COOKS SAY THESE ARE BEST FOR BAKING.

GOOSE EGGS LARGE WHITE-SHELLED EGGS THAT CAN WEIGH UP TO 300 G (10 OZ), THESE ARE IDEAL FOR OMELETTES OR SCRAMBLED EGGS.

QUAILS' EGGS TINY FAWN-COLOURED EGGS, PARTICULARLY ATTRACTIVE FOR CANAPES OR STARTERS.

POACHED EGGS WITH ANCHOVIES*

SERVES 4

2 × 50 g tins anchovies in oil, well drained
60 g (2 oz) butter, softened
4 large slices fresh white bread
vinegar
4 eggs (*see page 4 for advice on eggs)
cayenne pepper

*M*ake an anchovy butter by blending half the anchovies and the butter together in a blender or food processor. Bring a wide saucepan of boiling water to the boil.

Meanwhile, cut the crusts off the bread and make toast; keep warm. Add 1 teaspoon vinegar to the water and lower the temperature so it is just simmering. Slip in the eggs and poach for 5 minutes. Meanwhile, spread the toast generously with the anchovy butter.

Drain the eggs well with a slotted spoon and place 1 on each piece of toast. Top with a cross of anchovy fillets and sprinkle lightly with cayenne pepper. Serve at once.

SEAFOOD COCKTAILS*

A fairly recent English invention was the prawn cocktail, which soon became a very bad and very boring dish, so I have revived and improved it. The sauce in this recipe can be used with crab on its own, prawns on their own, or with lobster. It can be made a day ahead and assembled shortly before serving.

SERVES 8

500 g (1 lb) small uncooked prawns in their shells, defrosted if frozen
1 kg (2 lb) shelled scallops (about 2 scallops per person)
2 large tomatoes
1 head curly endive
at least 125 g (4 oz) lamb's lettuce

SAUCE

2 egg yolks (*see page 4 for advice on eggs)
1 generous teaspoon Dijon mustard
juice of 1 lemon
salt
300 ml (½ pint) sunflower oil
at least 2 teaspoons red wine
½ teaspoon tomato purée
2–3 shakes Tabasco sauce

COOKING THE SEAFOOD

Bring a wide pan of well-salted water to the boil, then lower the heat, drop in the prawns and simmer gently for 2–3 minutes. Lift the prawns out with a slotted spoon, then poach the scallops gently in the same liquid for 2–3 minutes, until just opaque. Scoop out with a slotted spoon and leave to cool.

Skin the tomatoes, cut in half and remove the seeds, then cut into small cubes.

Rinse the endive and lamb's lettuce carefully and shake dry. Choose only the best bits. Shell the prawns. Cut the scallops in half horizontally.

Arrange the shelled prawns, scallops, curly endive, lamb's lettuce and chopped tomato prettily on 8 dishes. Serve with the cocktail sauce.

TO MAKE THE SAUCE

Beat the egg yolks, mustard, lemon juice and salt together. When the mixture is light and creamy, add the oil steadily in a thin stream, whisking constantly, until all the oil is incorporated. Stir in the red wine, tomato purée and Tabasco sauce and whisk again. Cover and refrigerate until required.

GOLDEN BUTTER, EGGS, MILK AND CREAM ARE THE MAIN INGREDIENTS OF MANY EASILY PREPARED STARTERS.

DEVON POTTED SHRIMPS

These will keep well for a week in the refrigerator and are, in fact, improved after a few days. Lobster, crab and prawns can also be potted in exactly the same way, but do not keep longer than a day or two.

MAKES 6 SMALL POTS

500 lb (1 lb) shelled shrimps, fresh or frozen
250 g (8 oz) unsalted butter
½ teaspoon ground mace
¼ teaspoon cayenne pepper, or to taste
¼ teaspoon freshly ground black pepper
salt, if necessary
hot toast, to serve

*I*f the shrimps are frozen, let them defrost completely in a sieve so any melted ice drains off. They must be as dry as possible when you pour over the clarified butter.

To make the clarified butter, melt the butter in a small pan with a pouring lip, at the lowest temperature possible. Let it sit over this heat for 30 minutes, until all the whitish curds, which are the milk solids, have formed a layer at the bottom of the pan and the oily butter is quite clear.

Put the shrimps in a bowl and mix in the seasonings with your fingers. Pour on the clarified butter, leaving all the white solids in the pan. Wash out the solids and return clarified butter and shrimps to the pan and let it sit over the same very low heat for a further 30 minutes.

Divide the shrimps and butter between 6 small pots and press the shrimps down under the butter. Leave to set. Serve at room temperature with hot toast. If not serving at once, refrigerate until required.

SALMON MOUSSE*

You can make either a rough or smooth mousse. I find a rough mousse is more satisfactory as a main course, and a very fine one as a first course.

SERVES 6

500 g (1 lb) tail-end of salmon, poached (see page 53) with liquid reserved
½ teaspoon paprika
½ teaspoon Tabasco sauce
150 ml (¼ pint) home-made mayonnaise (see page 159)
15 g (½ oz) powdered gelatine
150 ml (¼ pint) reserved liquid in which the salmon was poached, or fish or chicken stock, hot
150 ml (¼ pint) whipping cream, whipped
salt and freshly ground white pepper
2 egg whites (*see page 4 for advice on eggs)
fresh dill, tarragon or parsley leaves, to garnish

*C*hop the salmon fairly finely, reserving 5 large, even flakes for garnishing. Stir the paprika and Tabasco into the mayonnaise.

Dissolve the gelatine in the hot stock, then leave it to cool but not set. Stir it gradually into the mayonnaise to make a smooth liquid. Stir in the salmon. At this point, if you are making a smooth mousse, purée the mixture thoroughly to a pink mousseline using a blender or food processor.

Stir in the whipped cream, and season generously. Whip the egg whites to a firm snow and fold carefully into the salmon mixture. Transfer to a 900 ml (1½ pint) soufflé dish and garnish the top with the reserved flakes of salmon and herb leaves. Cover and chill until set.

This mixture can also be divided among 6 or 8 small cocottes or ramekins and sprinkled with chopped fresh dill for individual servings.

As a starter, serve with hot toast or brown bread and butter, and quartered lemons or a bowl of mayonnaise with chopped dill and parsley stirred into it. As a main course, serve with a salad of lettuce hearts, fennel and thinly sliced radishes.

SALMON BUTTER

Spread this delicious soft pink butter lavishly on thin slices of toast for a quick starter, or even for tea or breakfast. Few things can be quicker to make.

MAKES ABOUT 250 g (8 oz)

180 g (6 oz) cooked salmon
90 g (3 oz) butter, softened
ground mace
sea salt

*R*emove every scrap of skin and bones from the salmon and discard, then pound the salmon flesh with a pestle and mortar until well mashed. Add the softened butter and continue pounding to a paste.

Season with a tiny pinch of mace – it is very strong – and a little sea salt. Cover and refrigerate if not using at once.

FRESHLY CAUGHT WILD SALMON ON THE SHORES OF LOCH LOMOND.

SALMON TROUT WITH HORSERADISH

Large farmed trout fed with special food which makes their flesh pink are now widely available. They are often passed off as salmon trout, and make a reasonable second-best. You can buy salmon trout already cleaned but check that all the black vein along the spine has been removed. If not, the fish will taste bitter.

SERVES 6

1 whole salmon trout, weighing
1.5–2 kg (3–4 lb)
salt
a little vegetable oil
2 tablespoons dry white wine
Horseradish Sauce (see page 158)

*P*reheat the oven to 170°C (325°F, Gas 3).

Rub the fish inside and out with salt, and coat with a little oil. Place a large piece of foil on a table or work surface and bend up the sides and ends. Put in the fish, sprinkle in the wine and fold the foil into a parcel, making sure the edges are folded over securely.

Bake for 30–40 minutes. Pierce the trout behind the head with a knife to see if it is cooked. A compact fish will take longer than a long thin one. When it is ready, remove it carefully, slide it on to a long dish and let it cool.

Serve with horseradish sauce.

VARIATIONS

Salmon trout cooked in foil is also extremely good served hot; the most usual sauce and one of the best is hollandaise (see page 53), but in early spring it is also rather good with a pink Maltaise sauce – hollandaise sauce with the juice of blood oranges incorporated.

A NOTE ON OPENING OYSTERS

PROVIDE YOURSELF WITH AN OYSTER KNIFE, TEA TOWELS AND A WIDE SHALLOW DISH. WRAP YOUR LEFT HAND IN A TEA TOWEL, HOLD AN OYSTER IN THE PALM OF THAT HAND, DEEP SHELL DOWNWARDS AND WITH THE HINGE TOWARDS YOU. INSERT THE BLADE OF THE OYSTER KNIFE INTO THE SIDE OF THE HINGE, FINDING A TINY HOLE OR CREVICE – NOT ALWAYS EASY – AND TWIST IT. CUT THE OYSTER OFF AND FLIP IT OVER SO THE PRETTY PLUMP SIDE IS ON DISPLAY.

OR, YOU CAN ASK THE FISHMONGER TO OPEN THE OYSTERS AND CARRY THEM HOME IN AN INSULATED BAG, THE SORT USED FOR PICNICS. POACH THE OYSTERS AS SOON AS YOU GET HOME. THEY CAN THEN BE TOPPED WITH THE SAUCE AND SPRINKLED WITH BREAD-CRUMBS AND REHEATED JUST BEFORE SERV-ING, BUT SHOULD BE EATEN WITHIN A COUPLE OF HOURS.

SCALLOPED OYSTERS IN THEIR SHELLS

Scalloped oysters certainly are very sweet and to my mind, the best; even people who do not like raw ones like these. I leave the oysters in their half-shells because they look so ravishingly pretty, whereas 6 oysters on a plate without their shells are very disappointing little things.

SERVES 4

45 g (1½ oz) butter
45 g (1½ oz) fresh breadcrumbs
24 oysters
6 tablespoons double cream
1 teaspoon freshly squeezed lemon juice
plenty cayenne pepper

*M*elt the butter and fry the bread-crumbs until golden and crisp. Shell the oysters (see left), keeping the deep halves of the shells, and enough of the liquid just to cover the oysters in a small pan. Pick out all the stray bits of shell, then bring the oysters to a simmer in their liquid. Remove them at once from the heat and strain them, reserving the liquid for the sauce. (Oysters shrink alarmingly if cooked for more than just a few seconds.) Wash the half shells and rinse well, then put an oyster in each.

Make a sauce with the cream, 4 table-spoons strained oyster cooking liquid, lemon juice and quite a lot of cayenne pepper. Let it simmer until it has reduced to a light but creamy texture. Meanwhile, preheat the grill or the oven to 170°C (325°F, Gas 3).

Taste for seasoning – it probably will not need salt – and pour some of this sauce over each oyster. Sprinkle each oyster with fried crumbs and heat through under the grill or in the oven. Serve at once, with bread to mop up the juices.

DUBLIN LAWYER

SERVES 2

This recipe is, as it sounds, Irish and comes from Theodora Fitzgibbon's *Irish Traditional Food*. I use Scotch whisky when I make this, and it is still sensationally good.

Cut 1 cooked lobster, weighing 750 g (1½ lb), in half and remove all the meat from the claws and shells, leaving the greenish tomalley in place.

Cut the lobster meat into 2 cm (¾ inch) pieces and put in a pan with 60 g (2 oz) butter over medium heat, stirring until all the pieces are coated. Light 2–3 tablespoon Irish whiskey in a ladle and pour it over. When the flames die down, remove the lobster meat with a slotted spoon, then stir 150 ml (¼ pint) double cream into the pan. Season with salt and cayenne pepper and boil about 3 minutes, until rich and creamy. Return the lobster and stir well, then serve piled back into the shells.

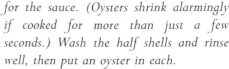

SCALLOPED OYSTERS IN THEIR SHELLS

CHICKEN OR VEAL STOCK

1 chicken carcass from a roast chicken,
or 1 small chicken, or 1 kg (2 lb) veal
knuckle bones
2 onions
2 leeks
2 sticks celery
3–4 sprigs fresh parsley
6 whole black peppercorns
salt
1 glass white wine (optional)

BEEF STOCK

250 g (8 oz) shin of beef
1 kg (2 lb) cracked beef bones
3 carrots
2 sticks celery
2–3 mushrooms, or a handful of
mushroom stalks and peelings
1 tomato
1 leek
2 onions in their skins
1 tablespoon butter
½ teaspoon salt
12 whole black peppercorns
1 bunch fresh herbs – thyme, parsley,
bay leaf

A WORD ABOUT THE STOCKPOT

THE OLD-FASHIONED STOCKPOT HAS GONE BY THE BOARD. TODAY, WE PREFER TO MAKE A FRESH-TASTING STOCK WITH FRESH INGREDIENTS AND USE IT WITHIN A DAY OR TWO, OR FREEZE IT TO USE LATER. THE REASONS FOR BOTHERING TO DO SUCH A THING AT ALL, WHEN USEFUL STOCK CUBES ARE SITTING IN THE CUPBOARD READY TO ADD ANY EXTRA FLAVOUR THAT A SOUP MAY REQUIRE, ARE NOT IMMEDIATELY CLEAR. BUT BY MAKING STOCK WITH FRESH VEGETABLES, A NEW FRESH FLAVOUR IS CREATED, SO EACH SOUP MADE AT HOME HAS A SUBTLY DIFFERENT TASTE – MUCH MORE INTERESTING THAN TASTING THE SAME CONCENTRATED STOCK CUBE FLAVOUR EVERY TIME, USEFUL THOUGH THEY MAY BE.

The simplest way to make this most useful of all stocks is to take the carcass, giblets and leftovers from a roast chicken as soon as you have eaten it, and put them into a saucepan of water with vegetables and herbs for flavour, and a glass of wine if you are using it. Let it simmer very slowly for 2 hours, then strain and cool quickly: the resulting delicate jellied stock will be useful for improving the flavour of all your sauces, soups and gravies.

A more classic recipe for white stock which has less flavour and sets to a firm jelly is made with a small chicken or veal bones. Place meat and bones in a large saucepan, cover with water and bring slowly to the boil, skimming well. Turn down the heat to a slow simmer, add the chopped vegetables, parsley and peppercorns and simmer slowly for 2 hours for chicken stock, 5 hours for veal stock. Season at the end, because the volume reduces considerably during the cooking. Strain through a fine sieve, leave to cool rapidly and place, covered, in the refrigerator where it will keep for 3 days. I like to boil some until it is very reduced and then freeze it in an ice-cube tray – making a home version of a stock cube. These keep up to 3 months in the freezer. This is applicable to all sorts of stock.

Chop the meat and all the vegetables, except the onions, into coarse chunks. Melt the butter in a large heavy-based pan and fry everything over a low heat, stirring from time to time, until the ingredients have absorbed the fat and become dark brown. The onions are fried whole in their skins to give the stock a beautiful golden colour. (You can add extra skins for a deeper brown-gold colour without spoiling the flavour – put them into the pan after the water has been added.)

Add enough cold water to cover, bring slowly to the boil, skim well and add salt, peppercorns and herbs, then lower the heat and simmer, covered with a tilted lid, for 3 hours. Sieve into a large bowl and chill; when cold remove fat, which will have solidified on top. You should have about 1.2 litres (2 pints) of excellent stock; it can be further reduced by gentle simmering to obtain a more concentrated, fuller-flavoured stock. Rapid boiling will turn it cloudy.

SUMMER CUCUMBER SOUP WITH DILL

Once it was considered very unhealthy to eat raw vegetables and even raw fruit – it was supposed to breed fevers, and cucumbers were particularly suspect – so early recipes are for cooked cucumber served in a soup, a ragout or as a vegetable. Cucumber is, in fact, excellent when cooked; I have combined cooked and raw cucumbers to get the nice flavour and velvetiness of cooked cucumber with the juiciness of a fresh one.

SERVES 6

2 cucumbers
1 onion
600 ml (1 pint) chicken stock, preferably home-made (see page 20)
1 glass dry white wine
1 bunch fresh herbs, including a dill sprig
salt and freshly ground white pepper
150 ml (¼ pint) plain yogurt
150 ml (¼ pint) soured cream, or more for a richer soup
1 bunch fresh dill
squeeze fresh lemon juice (optional)

*P*eel *and chop the cucumbers and onion. Put half the cucumber in a saucepan with the onion, chicken stock, white wine and bunch of herbs. Season with salt and freshly ground white pepper and bring to the boil, then skim and lower the heat and simmer for 20 minutes. Remove the bunch of herbs and purée the soup to a fine velvety texture.*

Transfer the soup to a bowl and leave it to cool. Purée the remaining cucumber with the yogurt and soured cream – do this very thoroughly to make certain the soup does not have too granular a texture.

Mix this raw cucumber mixture into the soup and taste for seasoning – it needs quite a lot of salt. Stir in the chopped dill and chill the soup until you are ready to serve it. Add a squeeze of lemon juice if you want a really sharp, refreshing soup.

THERE IS NO MORE PERFECT ACCOMPANIMENT TO HOME-MADE SOUPS THAN FRESHLY BAKED BREADS.

21

GARDEN VEGETABLE SOUP WITH HERBS

This soup is far less complicated than it appears, since you can include whatever green garden vegetables you like – green beans, spring onions and asparagus are also delicious. Cook the coarser ingredients first and then add the delicate ones towards the end of cooking.

SERVES 6

3 onions
½ small new turnip (optional)
2 small leeks
2 shallots
3–4 new potatoes
1 stick celery
1.5 litres (2½ pints) chicken stock,
preferably home-made (see page 20)
handful fresh spinach
1 bunch watercress
1 head lettuce
125 g (4 oz) shelled green peas
125 g (4 oz) shelled broad beans
salt and freshly ground black pepper
few tablespoons single or double cream
1 tablespoon finely chopped mixed
fresh chives, tarragon and parsley
croûtons (see page 27), to serve
(optional)

Wash and peel the onions, turnip, leeks, shallots and new potatoes. Cut them and the celery into even-sized pieces. Cook the vegetables in the stock for 15 minutes.

Meanwhile, rinse and pick over the spinach and watercress and shred the lettuce. Add these with the peas and broad beans to the pan, reserving a few leaves of watercress to garnish the soup. Cook for a further 10 minutes, then purée the soup in a blender or food processor. It should be a luscious green.

IF SERVING HOT

Strain the soup back into the rinsed-out pan, taste for seasoning and reheat. Serve with cream swirled through and a sprinkling of herbs on each serving. Tiny croûtons are also good with this.

IF SERVING COLD

Stir in the herbs and add the cream when the soup is cool. Serve at most lightly chilled and be sure to taste for seasoning again before serving: heavy chilling tends to make things tasteless.

GARDEN VEGETABLE SOUP WITH HERBS

VICHYSSOISE*

This traditional mid-Atlantic classic is as good hot as it is chilled.

SERVES 4–6

500 g (1 lb) leeks
1 onion
250 g (8 oz) potatoes
1 stick celery
few sprigs watercress
1 litre (1¾ pints) chicken stock,
preferably home-made (see page 20)
½ glass dry white wine
salt and freshly ground white pepper
1 egg yolk (*see page 4 for advice on
eggs)
150 ml (¼ pint) double cream
a few extra watercress leaves or 1
bunch chives

Prepare and cut up the vegetables and rinse and trim the watercress. Put the leeks, onion, potatoes and celery into a pan with the stock and white wine. Bring to the boil, season and cook for 10 minutes. Add the watercress and cook about 15 minutes, until tender.

Purée the soup through the fine blade of a food mill or in a blender or food processor and then sieve. Return the soup to the pan.

Put the egg yolk in a bowl and whisk it with a ladleful of the hot (not boiling) soup. Return this mixture to the pan and stir it into the rest of the soup together with about 5 tablespoons of the cream. Do not boil.

Cool the soup to room temperature and then chill, covered.

Give the soup a good stir, season and serve in bowls with a zig-zag pattern of the remaining cream in the centre – drizzle it on with a spoon in a thin stream – and 2 watercress leaves, or a sprinkling of chopped fresh chives.

MUSHROOMS

MANY VARIETIES OF MUSHROOMS ONCE ONLY AVAILABLE ABROAD OR IN THE WILD ARE NOW CULTIVATED IN BRITAIN, IN A HOST OF COLOURS, SHAPES AND SIZES. STORE IN THE REFRIGERATOR FOR NO MORE THAN 3 DAYS, AND JUST WIPE WITH A DAMP CLOTH, RATHER THAN SOAKING, BEFORE USING; BE SURE TO KEEP ANY TRIMMING FOR THE STOCKPOT.

BUTTON THE MOST POPULAR FUNGI IN BRITISH KITCHENS, THESE PEARLY WHITE MUSHROOMS HAVE A MILD FLAVOUR, EASILY OVERPOWERED BY OTHER INGREDIENTS. GOOD FOR EATING RAW.

CHESTNUT SIMILAR TO BUTTONS BUT WITH A THICKER STEM, ROUNDER, BROWNISH CAP AND STRONGER FLAVOUR. A GOOD GENERAL-PURPOSE VARIETY.

FLAT LARGE, MATURE CULTIVATED MUSH-ROOMS WITH A RICH FLAVOUR, OFTEN USED FOR STUFFING, GRILLING OR FRYING, SUCH AS IN MUSHROOMS IN CREAM, PAGE 121.

OYSTER FAN-SHAPED WITH A MILD FLAVOUR AND A TEXTURE THAT SOFTENS DURING COOKING. SAUTÉ AND ADD TO STEWS AND FRICASSEES TOWARDS THE END OF COOKING, OR FRY AND ADD TO SALADS.

MUSHROOM SOUP

SERVES 4–6

This recipe, like most soup recipes, is much improved by the use of good home-made chicken stock (see page 20); a stock cube, of course, will do, but leaves the soup somehow rather thin. You can also alter the richness by adding more or less cream and more or less nutmeg.

This soup is equally delicious either served hot or chilled – a rare, soft dove colour, and very fine. You can make this even more velvety by doubling the quantity of mushrooms and leaving out the potatoes entirely. A few wild mush-rooms, such as ceps or parasols, give it a more 'gamey' flavour. Freshly chopped chervil is the perfect herb to comple-ment the flavour of this soup, so I sometimes sprinkle some over the top just before serving.

1 large onion, plus 2 shallots if available
125 g (4 oz) potatoes
45 g (1½ oz) butter
375 g (12 oz) mushrooms
900 ml (1½ pints) chicken stock,
preferably home-made (see page 20),
or 600 ml (1 pint) chicken stock and
300 ml (½ pint) single cream
freshly grated nutmeg
salt and freshly ground black pepper
3–4 tablespoons double cream

Peel and chop the onion, shallots and potatoes coarsely, then soften them in the butter over a gentle heat for 15 minutes, stirring occasionally. Coarsely chop the mushrooms, add them and let them wilt and soften in the butter. Then add the stock, and season with plenty of nutmeg and salt and pepper.

Simmer the soup without boiling for 20 minutes or until everything is cooked, then leave it to cool a little before you purée it in a blender or food processor. Add the single cream at this point if you are using it, and taste for seasoning.

Either reheat, swirl in the double cream and serve hot, or let it cool and chill thoroughly before serving. If serving chilled, be sure to taste again for seasoning before serving.

ALMOND SOUP

Almonds used to be a great feature of British cookery, when they were toasted and used as a garnish and flavouring for green beans, or pounded and used to thicken sauces or to lighten cakes and puddings. In this recipe, almonds make a pearly and delicate soup.

SERVES 6

125 g (4 oz) ground almonds
300 ml (½ pint) milk
2 tablespoons fresh white breadcrumbs
30 g (1 oz) butter
30 g (1 oz) plain flour
1.2 litres (2 pints) chicken stock, preferably home-made (see page 20)
salt
cayenne pepper
ground mace
300 ml (½ pint) single cream
1 tablespoon butter
slivered almonds

Put the ground almonds with the milk in a small saucepan and simmer gently for 10 minutes. Add the crumbs and simmer for 3 minutes more, then purée in a blender or food processor or rub to a purée through a sieve with a spoon.

In a large pan, melt the butter, add the flour and stir it in, then stir in the almond purée. Gradually stir in the stock and when you have a smooth soup, season with salt, cayenne pepper and mace.

Simmer gently for 10 minutes, then remove from the heat and stir in the cream. Heat through gently. Meanwhile, melt the butter and fry the slivered almonds until golden brown, stirring. Scatter over the soup just before serving.

ENGLISH ONION SOUP

SERVES 4

4 large onions, or 6 small ones
2 sticks celery
60 g (2 oz) butter
60 g (2 oz) plain flour
300 ml (½ pint) milk
900 ml (1½ pint) chicken stock, preferably home-made (see page 20)
salt and freshly ground black pepper
freshly grated nutmeg
2 tablespoons chopped fresh parsley
4 tablespoons single cream

Peel and chop the onions and celery and cook them in a covered pan in a little butter and 1 tablespoon water for about 10 minutes, until they are very soft. Then purée the vegetables in a blender or a food processor or a food mill.

Keep the purée on one side while you melt the butter in the rinsed-out saucepan and stir in the flour to make a roux. When the flour and butter have combined and become smooth and glossy, add the milk, a little at a time, stirring constantly until you have a smooth mixture. Add the onion and celery purée and enough stock to make a smooth, creamy soup.

Simmer for 10 minutes, taste for seasoning, add a little nutmeg, stir in the parsley and lastly enrich the soup by pouring the cream into the middle of each serving and letting it swirl up to the top.

CREAM OF WATERCRESS SOUP

SERVES 4

2 bunches watercress
250 g (8 oz) onions
180 g (6 oz) floury potatoes, such as King Edward
½ stick celery
45 g (1½ oz) butter
150 ml (¼ pint) dry white wine
750 ml (1¼ pints) chicken stock, preferably home-made (see page 20)
150 ml (¼ pint) double cream
salt and freshly ground black pepper
extra butter (optional)
whipped cream (optional)

Pick all the best leaves from the tops of the watercress and set them aside.

Wash the stalks thoroughly and pick out any yellow or dead leaves. Peel and chop the onions and potatoes. Chop the celery.

Melt the butter in a fairly large pan and soften the onions and celery for several minutes over a low heat, without browning. Add the potatoes and the white wine, let it bubble up and then add the chicken stock. Cook for 10 minutes, add the watercress stalks and cook for a further 20 minutes, until everything is very tender.

Allow to cool a little, then reduce to a fine purée in a blender or food processor. Sieve and return the soup to the pan.

Chop the reserved watercress leaves fairly coarsely and add them to the soup. Cook for a few minutes, then stir in the cream. Taste for seasoning and heat through. Serve plain or with either a small knob of butter or a spoonful of whipped cream in each bowl, and a quantity of very coarsely ground pepper on top of that.

LEEK AND BACON SOUP

Leeks and bacon are always good together – this soup is enough for a complete lunch with brown bread and butter, thickly cut and thickly spread.

SERVES 6

2–3 leeks
1 onion
2 potatoes, about 250 g (8 oz)
2–3 rashers of your favourite bacon
45 g (1½ oz) butter
30 g (1 oz) plain flour
1.2 litres (2 pints) chicken stock,
preferably home-made (see page 20)
salt and freshly ground black pepper
300 ml (½ pint) milk
1–2 tablespoons single or double cream
chopped fresh parsley

*C*ut the leeks in half lengthways and rinse them well between the leaves. Cut crossways into 1 cm (½ inch) slices. Peel and chop the onion and cut the potatoes into cubes. Cut the bacon into 1 cm (½ inch) pieces.

Put the leeks and onion into a large pan with the bacon and butter and soften gently, without browning, for 5 minutes. Add the potatoes and stir them round, then stir in the flour. When it is well mixed in, add 300 ml (½ pint) stock and stir until smooth and thick. Then add the remaining stock, bring to the boil, lower the heat and simmer for 20 minutes.

Taste for seasoning, stir in the milk and, if you find the soup too thin, sieve some of it through a food mill or purée it in a blender or food processor. Return the purée to the soup.

To serve, reheat, stirring, then add a little cream and some chopped parsley.

LEEK AND BACON SOUP

LETTUCE SOUP WITH CREAM AND EGG YOLKS*

SERVES 6

2 heads lettuce – any firm type, such as
Little Gem and Crisphead
1 onion, or 2–3 shallots
30 g (1 oz) butter
1 litre (1¾ pints) chicken stock,
preferably homemade (see page 20)
1 glass dry white wine
1 bunch celery tops, chervil, parsley,
green onion tops (keep some fresh to
scatter on top of soup), tied together
2–3 egg yolks (*see page 4 for advice on
eggs)
salt and freshly ground white pepper
squeeze lemon juice, to taste
150 ml (¼ pint) double cream

*S*hred the lettuces, reserving 2 or 3 of the pale leaves from the heart. Chop the onion or shallots and soften them in the butter, without browning.

Wilt the lettuces down with the onion, then add the chicken stock, wine and bunch of flavourings and simmer 15–20 minutes, until everything is tender. Remove the bunch of flavourings. Purée the soup and strain back into the rinsed-out saucepan through a fine sieve.

Beat the egg yolks in a bowl and add a ladleful of the hot – not boiling – soup. Whisk together well, then transfer back to the pan. Taste for seasoning and add a little lemon juice if you like. Whip the cream to a soft light foam.

Heat the soup gently without boiling, stirring constantly. Stir in the whipped cream and serve scattered with very thin julienne strips of lettuce leaves and chopped spring onion tops.

In summer, the soup can be garnished with blue borage flowers and chives.

CROÛTONS

THE TRADITIONAL HABIT OF SERVING SIZZLING HOT CROÛTONS WITH SOUP MAKES SENSE. THEY PROVIDE SOMETHING CRISP TO COUNTERACT THE SMOOTHNESS OF THE SOUP. TO MAKE THEM, CUT BREAD INTO .5 CM (¼ INCH) CUBES AND FRY THESE IN BUTTER AND OIL UNTIL GOLDEN BROWN. DRAIN THEM WELL ON KITCHEN PAPER. IF MADE IN ADVANCE, CROÛTONS CAN BE REHEATED; THEY SHOULD BE SERVED SO HOT THAT THEY SIZZLE WHEN YOU SPOON THEM INTO THE HOT SOUP.

YELLOW PEA SOUP

SERVES 6

300 g (10 oz) yellow split peas
1 ham bone with a bit of ham on it, or
a raw gammon knuckle, soaked for
several hours
1 onion, chopped
1 stick celery, chopped
1 bay leaf
large pinch of dried marjoram
15 g (½ oz) butter
15 g (½ oz) plain flour
150 ml (¼ pint) milk
salt and freshly ground black pepper
150 ml (¼ pint) single cream

Soak the peas overnight in 1 litre (1¾ pints) water. (Or, if you are in a hurry, use the quicker method – cover the peas with 1 litre (1¾ pints) cold water, bring to the boil and cook for 5 minutes; cover the pan, remove from the heat and leave to cool.) If necessary, soak the ham bone – an uncooked smoked knuckle needs overnight soaking, a cooked bone will not.

Put the peas and their soaking water, the onion, celery, ham bone, bay leaf and pinch of marjoram in a large pan. Cover with 1.3 litres (2¼ pints) water and simmer for 1½–2 hours, until the peas are soft. Remove the bone and bay leaf and sieve through a food mill, or purée in a blender or food processor and then rub through a sieve.

Melt the butter in a small pan, stir in the flour and continue stirring for 2 minutes, then gradually stir in the milk. Cook over a low heat, stirring constantly until smooth and thickened. Stir into the soup, taste for seasoning and add half the cream. Remove the ham from the bone and cut it in small pieces, then add these to the soup. Heat through and serve with a swirl of cream and some very coarsely ground pepper on each bowlful.

LIGHT CARROT SOUP

I make this soup with young carrots which are somewhat mealy in texture if well cooked. Old carrots might not be so effective. As the soup contains no potatoes, it is very light, smooth and delicate. Half a teaspoon of cumin powder fried with the vegetables gives an interesting flavour, and you could spice it even more by using Garam Masala (see page 32), and scattering chopped coriander leaves over the soup before serving.

SERVES 4

375 g (12 oz) new carrots
1 large onion
1 stick celery
15 g (½ oz) butter
1 cm (½ inch) piece fresh root ginger, peeled
½ chilli, stem and seeds removed
600 ml (1 pint) chicken stock, preferably home-made (page 20)
300 ml (½ pint) milk
salt
dash single or double cream

Clean the carrots and chop them up. Chop the onion and celery and soften them gently in the butter for several minutes. Slice the ginger and chilli, then add the carrots, ginger and chilli to the pan and stir them round for 1 minute.

Stir in the chicken stock, bring to the boil, lower the heat and simmer until everything is very tender, about 25 minutes.

Purée in a food mill, blender or food processor and return the soup to the rinsed-out pan. Add the milk and season to taste with salt. Heat through and serve with a dash of cream or a thin trickle of cream dribbled over the top of the soup in a decorative pattern.

ENGLISH TOMATO AND MINT SOUP

It is crucial to use really good, ripe, rich tomatoes for this soup. I find a delicious alternative to fresh mint is fresh basil leaves.

SERVES 4

1 onion
1 small potato, peeled
1 leek
1 small stick celery (optional)
30 g (1 oz) butter
750 g (1½ lb) tomatoes, skinned
300 ml (½ pint) chicken stock, preferably home-made (see page 20)
a few sprigs fresh mint
up to 150 ml (¼ pint) double cream
salt and freshly ground black pepper

Chop the onion, potato, leek and celery and soften them well in the butter but don't let them brown. Keeping 2 bright red tomatoes aside, chop the remainder, crush them with a potato masher and add them to the other vegetables. Pour the stock into the pan, bring to the boil, then lower the heat and leave to simmer for 20–25 minutes, stirring occasionally.

Meanwhile, cut the remaining tomatoes in half and squeeze out the pips, then cut the flesh into dice. Chop the mint.

When the soup is cooked, purée it in a food mill, blender or food processor and strain through a fine sieve. Return the soup to the rinsed-out pan and stir in the double cream (single cream may curdle). Heat through, taste for seasoning, stir in the diced raw tomatoes and chopped mint and serve.

ENGLISH TOMATO AND MINT SOUP (TOP);
LIGHT CARROT SOUP

MUSSEL CHOWDER

This hearty, filling soup is more like a main course than a starter. Simply serve it with chunks of good brown bread.

SERVES 6

2 kg (4 lb) mussels
1 large onion, finely chopped
60 g (2 oz) butter
125 g (4 oz) smoked streaky bacon, cut into small strips
4 potatoes, cut in cubes
45 g (1½ oz) plain flour
600 ml (1 pint) milk mixed with 450 ml (¾ pint) water
3–4 sprigs fresh parsley, chopped
salt and freshly ground black pepper
2–3 tablespoons double cream or more

*D*iscard any opened mussels. Clean the mussels, removing the beards with a small knife and scrubbing the shells if necessary. Any barnacles can be knocked off with the back of a knife blade.

Soften the onion in the butter in a large heavy-based saucepan together with the bacon. When the onions are pale yellow and transparent, but not brown, add the potatoes, stirring them round for a few moments. Add the flour, and stir this in, too.

Gradually, stir in the milk and water, stirring until you have a creamy soup, adding more water if necessary. Simmer for 5 minutes. Throw in the mussels, cover the pan, bring to the boil and let them cook for 4–5 minutes, stirring once or twice, until they have all opened; discard any that remain closed. Add the chopped parsley, taste for seasoning and lastly add the cream. Stir and serve.

ALWAYS USE FRESH HERBS, RATHER THAN DRIED, FOR FLAVOURING SOUPS.

RICH CREAM OF CHICKEN SOUP*

This soup should be delicate, white and pure, with a good flavour of chicken, so I suggest you use a whole bird.

SERVES 4–6

2 sticks celery
2 onions
1 leek
legs, carcass and giblets of a chicken (the breasts can be used in another recipe), or much better use a whole chicken, young or old
8 whole black peppercorns
1 sprig fresh thyme
1 bunch fresh parsley
4 egg yolks (*see page 4 for advice on eggs)
150 ml (¼ pint) double or single cream
salt

*S*lice the celery, onions and leek and put in a large pan with the carcass, legs and giblets (except the liver). Add the peppercorns and herbs, tied up in an outer leaf from the leek, and 2.4–3 litres (4–5 pints) cold water. Bring to a simmer and skim carefully; keep skimming from time to time for as long as fat and impurities continue to rise to the top. Let the liquid just tremble for 2 hours, then strain it carefully through a clean tea towel and return it to the rinsed-out pan. Simmer slowly, uncovered, until reduced to 1.2 litres (2 pints). Taste for seasoning.

Beat the egg yolks with the cream and season lightly with salt. Ladle in a few tablespoons of the hot – not boiling – soup and stir well. Off the heat, add the egg and cream mixture to the pan, then return to a low heat and whisk until smooth. Do not allow to boil. Taste for seasoning and serve at once.

EMERALD SPINACH SOUP

Cooking the spinach in butter, rather than in the soup itself, gives the finished a particularly good, velvety texture and an attractive deep green colour.

SERVES 4–6

500 g (1 lb) fresh spinach
1 onion
1 shallot
1 leek
1 potato
60 g (2 oz) butter
75 ml (3 fl oz) dry white wine
1.2 litres (2 pints) chicken stock, preferably home-made (see page 20)
salt and freshly ground black pepper
freshly grated nutmeg
60 ml (2 fl oz) whipping cream, whipped

*R*inse and pick over the spinach, tearing out and discarding any yellow patches, then leave it in a colander to drain. Shred 6 young leaves and keep them aside. Chop the onion, shallot and leek finely. Peel and grate the potato.

Melt half the butter and soften the chopped onion, shallot and leek; add the grated potato, wine and the stock and cook gently for 20 minutes, stirring occasionally, until tender. Season to taste with salt, pepper and nutmeg. Set the soup aside.

Cook the spinach in the remaining butter until it wilts down, adding it to the pan a few handfuls at a time. Add it to the soup, bring to the boil for 1 minute, then remove from the heat and purée in a blender or food processor.

Serve the soup hot with a few shreds of spinach and a dollop of whipped cream on top of each serving.

CURRIED LENTIL SOUP

This is a sort of Mulligatawny but rather more subtle. As an alternative, it can also be made with other varieties of lentil, or with split yellow peas. Make the special stock if you have time as it gives the soup a most delicious flavour; if not use vegetable or chicken stock.

SERVES 6

SPECIAL STOCK

500 g (1 lb) stewing beef, such as shin
2 carrots
1 onion, stuck with a clove
1 stick celery
1 bay leaf
1 sprig fresh lovage
½ teaspoon whole black peppercorns

SOUP

1 carrot
1 stick celery
1 onion
4 cloves garlic, peeled
45 g (1½ oz) butter
250 g (8 oz) small split orange lentils
1 tablespoon garam masala (left)
1.8 litres (3 pints) stock (see above)
1 teaspoon curry paste
4 cardamom pods
150 ml (¼ pint) double cream, plus extra for serving
milk, to taste
salt
chopped fresh coriander

TO MAKE THE SPECIAL STOCK

Cover the stock ingredients with water and bring to the boil. Lower the heat, skim and simmer 3–4 hours. Strain and make up to 1.8 litres (3 pints) with water.

TO MAKE THE SOUP

Chop the vegetables and slice the cloves of garlic. Melt the butter in a large pan and add the lentils, chopped vegetables, garlic and garam masala. Stir them round for a few minutes, but don't allow to brown.

Stir in the stock, curry paste and cardamom pods. Simmer for 45 minutes–1 hour, until the lentils and vegetables are tender. Purée in a food mill, blender or food processor – if using the latter, strain the soup through a sieve.

Stir in the cream and enough milk to give the consistency you like. Taste for seasoning and serve very hot with 1 teaspoon of cream in each soup plate, and a scattering of chopped fresh coriander.

NOTE

If you do not have time to make the garam masala, 1 teaspoon ground coriander and ½ teaspoon ground cumin can be added to an ordinary curry powder.

HOTCH POTCH

SERVES 4–6

2 onions
2 carrots
1 slice white turnip, peeled
1.8 litres (3 pints) lamb broth from a boiled leg of lamb
1 head lettuce
1 small head green cabbage
250 g (8 oz) shelled green peas
1 tablespoon chopped fresh parsley
coarsely ground black pepper

Cut the onions, carrots and turnip into small pieces and put them in a pan with the broth. Bring to the boil, then lower the heat and simmer with a tilted lid on the pan for 30 minutes.

Add the lettuce and the cabbage, shredded, and simmer for 30 minutes. Add the peas and cook, uncovered, for 10 minutes, then add the parsley and lots of very coarse and freshly ground black pepper.

GARAM MASALA

BRITISH COOKS HAVE A LONG TRADITION OF MAKING THEIR OWN VERSION OF INDIAN CURRY. IN INDIA, HOWEVER, YOU WILL NOT FIND CURRY POWDER ON KITCHEN SHELVES, BUT YOU WILL FIND THIS SPICY MIXTURE. USED ON ITS OWN OR IN ADDITION TO CURRY POWDER OR YOUR OWN BLEND OF SPICES, GARAM MASALA GIVES AN AROMATIC LIFT TO PLAIN OR SIMPLE DISHES. UNLIKE CURRY POWDER, WHICH NEEDS TO BE COOKED, THIS CAN BE SPRINKLED OVER THE TOP TOWARDS THE END OF COOKING.

USING A CLEAN COFFEE GRINDER OR PESTLE AND MORTAR, GRIND TO A POWDER 2 TABLESPOONS CUMIN SEEDS, 1 TABLESPOON WHOLE BLACK PEPPERCORNS, 16 CRUSHED CLOVES AND 4 CRUSHED CARDAMOM PODS (HUSKS REMOVED). SIEVE AND STORE IN AN AIR-TIGHT CONTAINER. THIS MAKES ABOUT 5 TABLESPOONS.

PARSLEY-BARLEY BROTH

SERVES AT LEAST 6

125 g (4 oz) yellow split peas
2 onions
3 carrots
1 small turnip
1 small swede (optional)
90 g (3 oz) pearl barley
1.8 litres (3 pints) beef or lamb stock
1 young leek
1 tender white inner stick celery
1 small slender parsnip (optional)
¼ fresh green cabbage
salt and freshly ground pepper
2–3 tablespoons chopped fresh parsley

*S*oak the split peas overnight. Alternatively, put them in a saucepan of cold water, bring to the boil, lower the heat and simmer for 5 minutes. Remove them from the heat, cover the pan and leave to cool. By the time the peas are cool they are soft enough to cook. Drain off the soaking water.

Cut the onions, carrots, turnip and swede into small pieces and put them into a saucepan with the soaked peas and barley. Cover with the stock, bring to the boil, lower the heat, skim well and simmer for 1 hour.

Meanwhile, slice the leek into halves lengthwise and then into small pieces. Cut the celery into little crescents. Cut the parsnip into quarters and then slice it.

TRADITIONAL BRITISH COOKING EVOKES AN IMAGE OF COSY COUNTRY KITCHENS.

Add these to the soup and cook for a further 15–20 minutes.

Remove the stalk from the cabbage and slice into small and manageable strips – long strips are to be avoided as they hang over the side of the spoon and drip everywhere. Add the cabbage to the soup and simmer until all the vegetables are tender, adding more stock if necessary. Season.

Sprinkle with plenty of chopped parsley and coarsely ground black pepper at the last minute and serve very hot with bread and butter. The soup reheats well but becomes thick – add more stock if necessary.

LIGHT MEALS
AND SALADS

*D*uring the week very few people seem to want a large meal either at lunch or in the evening. There just isn't time. There are many times when people are rushing in and out frenetically and will perhaps eat something at some unspecified time. So this chapter consists of dishes which can be kept hot or made at the last moment. It also includes a soufflé, and several salads of the sort that can either be eaten on their own or with a meal. The recent arrival in the shops of a particularly good lettuce called Little Gem, and the fact that we can now get reasonably priced virgin olive oil and sherry vinegar have made a huge difference in the quality of ordinary green salad, so now there really is no excuse for serving a salad that is less than crisp, well flavoured and fresh.

SALMON HASH (PAGE 37)

PEPPERED EGGS WITH SMOKED SALMON*

Serve the eggs on a slice of toast if you like and be sure to put the smoked salmon on the side – if you put it over the top of hot eggs it will go oily and then start to lose its translucence.

SERVES 6

90 g (3 oz) butter
12 free-range eggs (*see page 4 for advice on eggs)
1 teaspoon salt
24–30 whole black peppercorns
6 slices smoked salmon

*H*alf-melt the butter over a low heat in a good thick saucepan. Remove from the heat and allow to cool, then add the eggs 1 at a time. Season with up to 1 teaspoon salt, less if using salted butter.

Pound the peppercorns roughly in a mortar with a pestle and add them to the eggs. Return the pan to the heat and stir, scraping the bottom of the pan continuously with a wooden spoon. The eggs will start to set and form lumps. Keep going until the eggs are about two-thirds set, then remove the pan from the heat and finish cooking, still stirring, in the cooling pan so you do not have any overcooked bits of eggs.

When the eggs are soft and creamy and

PEPPERED EGGS WITH SMOKED SALMON

cooked all the way through, divide among the plates alongside the smoked salmon and serve at once with more pepper for grinding over the tops of each. Do not serve lemon with this.

ALTERNATIVE

As an extremely delicious alternative, serve fillets of smoked eel with the scrambled eggs. Allow two 10 cm (4 inch) pieces of fillet to each person and put them in a cross over the top of the scrambled eggs – as they are thicker than smoked salmon slices they can stand up to the heat of the eggs without spoiling.

SALMON HASH

SERVES 4–6

2–3 potatoes
6 spring onions
45 g (1½ oz) butter
500 g (1 lb) left-over cold, cooked
salmon
salt and cayenne pepper

*B*oil the potatoes in their skins. Chop the spring onions and soften them in a little butter in a large frying pan.

Break the salmon into flakes and stir those into the spring onions with the peeled and diced potatoes and the remaining butter. Fry gently without breaking the fish or potatoes until nicely browned. Season with salt and cayenne pepper.

BREAKFAST KEDGEREE

This is a very good breakfast dish; it can be kept hot while people wander downstairs for a weekend perusal of the newspapers in their dressing-gowns, and it reheats well for anybody who has been out walking or gardening early, or stayed out late the night before.

SERVES 4

500 g (1 lb) smoked haddock fillets
300 ml (½ pint) milk
1 strip lemon rind
1 bay leaf
75 g (2½ oz) butter
3 eggs, hard-boiled
180 g (6 oz) basmati rice
salt and cayenne pepper

*P*reheat the oven to 190°C (375°F, Gas 5).

Cook the haddock in a buttered baking tin with the milk, lemon rind, bay leaf, 15 g (½ oz) butter and 150 ml (¼ pint)

water for 15 minutes. Leave to cool. Chop the hard-boiled eggs.

Cook the rice very lightly, either in salted water or, better, in the cooking liquid from the fish. Mix together the rice, which should be well drained, with the chopped eggs. Flake the haddock and gently stir it in. Add 60 g (2 oz) butter and heat through, tossing lightly with a fork. Sprinkle well with cayenne pepper, fork the kedgeree through once more and serve very hot.

VARIATION

To turn this into a richer, supper dish, cook the fish in all milk, instead of milk and water. Then use the fishy flavoured milk, with half the butter, 30 g (1 oz) plain flour and 1 teaspoon curry powder, to make a creamy sauce. Pour the sauce into the kedgeree and heat until it bubbles, then serve at once.

SOUSED HERRING

The point of soused herring is first and foremost that it makes a good summer lunch, but also that once soused the herring can be kept for several days.

MAKES 6

6 fresh herring, preferably with soft roes, weighing 180 g–250 g (6–8 oz) each
300 ml (½ pint) cider vinegar
300 ml (½ pint) dry cider
salt
4 bay leaves
4 sprigs fresh thyme
12 whole black peppercorns
4 cloves
2 blades mace

*P*reheat the oven to 180°C (350°F, Gas 4).

Scrape the scales off the herring. Cut off their tails and heads, clean them thoroughly reserving the soft roes, then rinse them again under the tap. Pat them dry, put back the roes and lay them in a large pie dish, heads to tails. Cover with the vinegar and dry cider. Strew the salt, herbs and spices over the top, cover with a sheet of oiled foil (this will prevent the smell from spreading) and stand the dish in a roasting tin of boiling water.

Bake for 30 minutes, then leave to cool. Chill until ready to serve.

Serve chilled, garnished with watercress and with a green salad with hard-boiled eggs chopped into it.

An alternative is to fillet the scaled herring, then roll up each fillet and secure with a toothpick, continuing as above.

DRESSED CRAB

Fresh crab has a much more luscious texture than frozen and far more flavour, so the performance needed to get it all out of its shell is more than worth the effort. I consider it as good as lobster. Choose a heavy crab; light crabs tend to be dry and wasted inside.

1 kg (2 lb) crab serves 1;
1.5–2 kg (3–4 lb) crab serves 2

*A*sk a fishmonger to loosen the body of the crab from the shell for you, to see it is a good fleshy crab, and to remove the gills which are also known as 'deadman's fingers' and are not edible.

With a wood mallet, hammer or a rolling pin, a skewer and a large wooden chopping board at the ready, open up the crab, pulling the slender legs and the lower body away from the top shell. Take all the brown meat from around the inside of the top shell and a few teaspoons more

from the centre of the crab's body. Put it into a bowl, season lightly with fresh black or cayenne pepper and a few drops of lemon juice and mash it with a fork until it is smooth. Taste and add salt, if it is needed.

Now crack the large claws and remove the white meat, flaking it into a separate bowl. Cut the body into 3 pieces with a large heavy knife and pick out the meat from all the little shell cavities with a skewer, taking care not to get pieces of shell into the bowl. On a large crab you can also break the long thin claws with your hands and extract the meat from these. Mix the white meat with a couple of tablespoons of mayonnaise, if liked.

Arrange the small crisp inner leaves of a Cos lettuce or endive all around a deep dish and pile the white meat in a ring around the edges. Put the brown meat in the centre. Serve with slices of brown bread and butter, quarters of lemon and a bowl of mayonnaise for those who like a richer dressed crab.

CHEESE AND POTATO SUPPER

This is a sort of last resort recipe, to make when there isn't much in the larder, and you don't want to go out. Soothing on its own, it is also good served with grilled lamb cutlets.

SERVES 5

1 kg (2 lb) potatoes
125 g (4 oz) Cheshire, Lancashire or Cheddar cheese or a bit more
butter
sea salt and freshly ground black pepper
150 ml (¼ pint) milk
1 bay leaf
2–3 onion slices

*P*reheat the oven to 180°C (350°F, Gas 4). Peel the potatoes and slice them into rounds each .3 cm (⅛ inch) thick. Coarsely grate the cheese.

Butter a 25 cm (10 inch) oval oven-proof dish and cover the bottom with a layer of sliced potatoes. Season and cover with a layer of cheese. Repeat the layering – you should be able to make about 4 layers of potatoes. Finish with a layer of cheese. Cover and bake for 30 minutes.

Meanwhile, pour the milk into a saucepan and add the bay leaf and 2–3 slices of onion. Heat through gently, and keep hot to infuse. After the potato and cheese layers have baked for 30 minutes, remove the dish from the oven and strain the hot milk over them. Return the dish to the oven for a further 30–40 minutes, by which time the potatoes should have absorbed the milk and be tender all the way through.

FARMHOUSE CHEESES AND FRUIT MAKE AN UNBEATABLE LIGHT MEAL. THIS SELECTION INCLUDES RED LEICESTER, TWO STILTONS AND CHEDDAR.

REGIONAL CHEESES

A RENEWED INTEREST IN BRITISH REGIONAL CHEESES MEANS MORE PEOPLE APPRECIATE THE VARIED FLAVOURS AND TEXTURES. WHETHER YOU BUY CHEESE FRESHLY CUT OR WRAPPED, IT SHOULD NOT LOOK DRY AND CRACKED OR BE OILY. HOWEVER, A BIT OF MOULD IS QUITE NATURAL.

CAERPHILLY FROM WALES, THIS PALE CRUMBLY CHEESE'S MILD, SLIGHTLY ACIDIC FLAVOUR IS BEST APPRECIATED RAW IN SALADS AND SANDWICHES RATHER THAN IN COOKED DISHES.

CHEDDAR THE KING OF BRITISH CHEESE THAT IS COPIED AROUND THE WORLD. ITS FULL FLAVOUR PROGRESSES FROM MILD WHEN YOUNG TO NUTTY AND SHARP WHEN MATURE. AN ALL-PURPOSE CHEESE, CHEDDAR IS EXCELLENT FOR EATING, GRATING, COOKING, IN SANDWICHES AND SALADS AND FOR SERVING WITH WINE. TRADITIONALLY MADE FARMHOUSE CHEESES WILL BE STORED AT LAST NINE MONTHS, WHILE FACTORY-PRODUCED 'MILD' CHEDDAR IS MATURED FOR 3 TO 5 MONTHS AND 'MATURE' IS OFTEN SOLD AFTER 5 MONTHS.

CHESHIRE A CRUMBLY RED CHEESE, WITH A NUTTY AND SALTY TASTE, HAS A REPUTATION AS ONE OF EUROPE'S BEST COOKING CHEESES, MAKING IT IDEAL FOR A CHEESE AND POTATO SUPPER, LEFT. ALSO AVAILABLE IS THE SHARP WHITE VARIETY AND OCCASIONALLY A BLUE.

LEICESTER THE VEGETABLE COLOUR ANNATTO GIVES THIS CHEESE ITS INSTANTLY RECOGNIZABLE RUSSET-ORANGE COLOUR. THE SWEET, NUTTY TASTE MAKES IT A GOOD ADDITION TO ANY CHEESEBOARD, AND IT IS PERFECT FOR TOASTING OR USING IN SAUCES.

STILTON OFTEN FORGOTTEN EXCEPT AT CHRISTMAS, THIS CREAMY, VEINED CHEESE IS DELICIOUS EATEN RAW WITH A STICK OF CRISP CELERY AND A FEW WALNUTS OR CRUMBLED INTO A GREEN SALADS. COOKED, IT IS USEFUL IN SOUPS AND ADDS A SOPHISTICATED TASTE TO THE WELSH RABBIT OF STILTON AND WALNUTS (SEE PAGE 44).

WENSLEYDALE THE WHITE VARIETY OF THIS FLAKY CHEESE IS THE ONE AND ONLY CHEESE, ACCORDING TO YORKSHIREMEN, TO EAT WITH APPLE PIE. BLUE WENSLEYDALE IS DIFFICULT TO FIND, BUT WORTH THE EFFORT.

OMELETTE ARNOLD BENNETT*

SERVES 4

2 whole Finnan haddock, weighing
350 g (12 oz) each, or 1 large one
weighing 750 g (1½ lb)
300 ml (½ pint) milk
30 g (1 oz) butter
6 eggs (*see page 4 for advice on eggs)
45–60 g (1½–2 oz) finely grated cheese –
a mixture of Cheddar, Gruyère and
Parmesan is ideal
salt
150 ml (¼ pint) double cream

Preheat the oven to 170°C (325°F, Gas 3).

Put the haddock face downwards in a small roasting tin with the milk and a little water. Dot with a few nuts of the butter and bake in the oven for 15–20 minutes, until just cooked through. Leave the fish to become cool enough to handle, then remove all the bones and the skin. Flake the fish into a bowl.

Beat the eggs together and stir them into the haddock, together with all but 1 tablespoon or so of the cheese. Taste the mixture and add a little salt if necessary. Whip the cream and preheat the grill.

Heat 1 tablespoon of butter in a frying pan and, when it starts to brown, pour in the egg mixture. Cook for a few minutes and move the mixture around with a palette knife so it does not burn. When the bottom is set, put the frying pan under the grill until the top is all but set. Then spread the cream over the top, sprinkle with the remaining grated cheese and glaze to a beautiful flecked golden brown under the grill.

Serve the omelette hot, cut in wedges like a cake. I find this omelette is also delicious cold.

WELSH RABBIT OF STILTON AND WALNUTS

People are often left with large amounts of Stilton to eat their way through after Christmas; this is one easy way of doing it. Not everybody knows how good Stilton is served hot, melting and overflowing the edges of a piece of fresh toast.

To make this extremely delicious dish, toast a piece of bread on one side, butter the untoasted side lightly and crumble over 30 g (1 oz) Stilton. Scatter the contents of 3 fresh walnuts over the top. Grill very gently until the Stilton starts to run, then serve at once.

CHICKEN SALAD

SERVES 6

1 freshly roasted chicken, cooled and chilled
150 ml (¼ pint) home-made mayonnaise
(see page 159), flavoured with lemon juice
1 teaspoon hot curry powder
1 teaspoon lemon juice
2–3 tablespoons lightly whipped cream
salt and freshly ground black pepper
4 long sprigs fresh tarragon, chopped

You can either take the chicken off the bones or cut it into joints. Make sure it is completely cool or it will melt the mayonnaise and the salad will be rather limp. Put the meat into a bowl.

Mix the lemon juice, curry powder and cream into the mayonnaise and taste for seasoning. Stir in the chopped tarragon, then pour it over the chicken. Turn the pieces over until they are coated. Serve with lettuce hearts and cold rice and with mango chutney, if you like.

WELSH RABBIT OF STILTON AND WALNUTS

SALAD GREENS

THERE HAS NEVER BEEN SUCH A WONDERFUL SELECTION OF INGREDIENTS FOR THE SALAD BOWL. GREENHOUSE GROWERS AND RAPID TRANSPORTATION SYSTEMS PROVIDE GREENS THAT WERE ONCE PROHIBITIVELY EXPENSIVE OR ONLY AVAILABLE ON A TRIP ABROAD. I MIX THESE 'NEW' GREENS WITH OLD FAVOURITES.

CHICORY THERE IS NO MISTAKING THE BITTER TASTE OF THIS PALE, TIGHTLY PACKED CONE-SHAPED VEGETABLE. THE SOFT, YET CRISP, LEAVES CAN BE ADDED WHOLE TO A SALAD, OR SLICED; IT IS ALSO DELICIOUS COOKED. AVOID ANY LOOSE HEADS OR THOSE STARTING TO TURN BROWN ON THE TIPS; STORE UP TO 3 DAYS IN THE FRIDGE. IN DAYLIGHT, THEY RAPIDLY TURN BITTER.

FRISÉE A MEMBER OF THE CHICORY FAMILY, THIS LOOKS LIKE A FRIZZY OPEN LETTUCE WITH BRIGHT GREEN-TIPPED LEAVES AND A PALE CENTRE. AS WELL AS ITS BITTER TASTE, FRISÉE ADDS A CRISP TEXTURE. IT NEEDS A STRONG-FLAVOURED DRESSING. STORE UP TO 3 DAYS IN THE FRIDGE.

LAMB'S LETTUCE THESE SOFT DARK GREEN LEAVES HAVE A DISTINCTIVE SWEET NUTTY FLAVOUR THAT PERKS UP ANY SALAD; USEFUL IN WINTER WITH BEETROOT. THE LEAVES USUALLY NEED A GOOD RINSING AND SHOULD NOT BE KEPT MORE THAN 1 DAY.

LITTLE GEM LOOKING LIKE A MINIATURE COS, THIS SMALL LETTUCE HAS BEEN POPULAR IN HOME GARDENS SINCE THE TURN OF THE CENTURY, BUT ONLY RECENTLY GROWN ON A COMMERCIAL SCALE. THE COMPACT HEAD HAS A DENSE HEART AND CRISP TEXTURE. STORE IN THE FRIDGE UP TO 3 DAYS.

RADICCHIO THIS GARNET-RED ITALIAN CHICORY HAS BEEN VERY MUCH IN VOGUE FOR THE PAST COUPLE OF YEARS, ADDING BOTH COLOUR AND A BITTER FLAVOUR TO SALADS. DO NOT BUY DULL-LOOKING HEADS OR ANY STARTING TO BROWN. STORE WELL WRAPPED IN THE REFRIGERATOR UP TO 3 DAYS.

WATERCRESS ADDS A SHARP, PEPPERY TASTE TO SALADS. DO NOT BUY ANY STARTING TO TURN YELLOW, AND USE WITHIN 1 DAY. STORE IN THE REFRIGERATOR IN ITS PACKET, OR LEAVES DOWN IN A BOWL OF WATER. IT HAS AN AFFINITY WITH FISH, AND IS GOOD AS A SOUP (SEE PAGE 25).

SUMMER SALAD WITH FLOWERS

To make this a salad everyone will appreciate and remember, it is important to keep the vegetables whole or in very large quarters; once you have started cutting them into little pieces you will end up with nothing more or less than a mean and boring Russian salad.

Fill a bowl with a selection of blanched and cooled vegetables. Young and tender peas straight from the garden are ideal, but don't stop there. Other suitable ingredients include a few mushrooms, tiny new potatoes, French beans, very young carrots, asparagus tips and even artichoke bottoms.

Generously coat the vegetables with a fairly loose mayonnaise (see page 4 for advice on eggs if you use home-made mayonnaise), then spoon on top of a serving platter or bowl lined with lettuce leaves. Garnish with young and crisp nasturtium flowers and bright blue borage blossoms.

Serve accompanied by a plate of sliced tomatoes dressed with an oil and vinegar dressing and plenty of freshly ground black pepper.

SORREL SALAD

SERVES 4

Rich Salad Dressing (see page 159)
2 crisp lettuces, such as Little Gem,
with nice yellow hearts
3 handfuls young sorrel leaves
3 eggs, hard-boiled

*P*ut the salad dressing in the bottom of the salad bowl. Put the salad servers side by side, ends crossed, in the bowl, so that they slightly cover the dressing – this stops the salad from going soggy while it sits and waits for its moment to come.

Throw away all the outer leaves of lettuce, don't keep any that are coarse or dark coloured. Separate the inner leaves and put them into the salad bowl, on top of the salad servers. Put the sorrel on top.

Chop the hard-boiled eggs very coarsely and put them on top of this. Toss the salad really well at the last moment just before serving. It is very delicious with cold salmon or after any sort of fish.

WATERCRESS, CHICORY AND HAZELNUT SALAD

SERVES 6

2 bunches large-leaved watercress
3 heads chicory
45 g (1½ oz) hazelnuts
Best Salad Dressing (see page 159)

*W*ash the watercress and remove the hairy stalks and any dead or badly damaged leaves. Shake the leaves dry in a cloth or a salad spinner.

Remove the outside leaves from the chicory and slice lengthwise into quarters and then into eighths. Slice the hazelnuts downwards into 3 or 4 little round slices and toast them lightly in a heavy frying pan until they are golden brown.

Arrange the chicory sticking up all the way round the salad bowl and put the watercress in the middle. Scatter the nuts on top of the watercress. Pour on the dressing at the last moment just before serving and toss the salad until all the leaves are thoroughly coated.

LAMB'S LETTUCE AND BEETROOT SALAD

In the winter this is one of the most excellent and well-flavoured salads you can make. If you grow lamb's lettuce this is the best way to eat it. If there are good avacodoes available, I sometimes make this salad with Rich Salad Dressing (see page 159) to add extra flavour and texture. This is extremely good served with roast lamb or beef, or with game.

SERVES 6

250 g (8 oz) lamb's lettuce
2 beetroots, cooked without vinegar
(about 125 g/4 oz each; the large ones
have less flavour)
Best Salad Dressing (see page 159)

*R*inse the lamb's lettuce in a large basin of cold water, shaking each little bunch of leaves about in the water to get all the grit out. Nip off the root with your finger and thumbnails and drain the leaves in a colander. Then shake gently but thoroughly in a cloth or salad shaker. Transfer the lamb's lettuce to the salad bowl.

Skin the beetroots, cut them in quarters and then slice thickly. Scatter the pieces over the top of the lamb's lettuce.

Dress with the well-flavoured, thick dressing at the table.

LAMB'S LETTUCE AND BEETROOT SALAD WITH
RICH SALAD DRESSING (PAGE 159) (TOP);
SUMMER SALAD WITH FLOWERS

SALMON KEDGEREE

SERVES 4

250 g (8 oz) fresh salmon in 1 piece
salt and freshly ground black pepper
30 g (1 oz) butter
250 g (8 oz) basmati rice
3 eggs, size 1
125 g (4 oz) shelled peas (fresh or
frozen)
150 ml (¼ pint) double cream
2 tablespoons chopped fresh parsley

A good traditional British way to cook a slice or cutlet of fish is to salt it and put it with a little butter – 15–30 g (½–1 oz) – between 2 plates. These are put over a pan of cooking rice and the fish poaches gently in its own steam and juices. A slice of salmon weighing 250 g (8 oz) takes about the same time as the rice.

To cook the rice, rinse it and put it in a pan with 300 ml (½ pint) water and a generous pinch of salt. Bring it to the boil, then stir it once and cover the pan. Simmer for 15–20 minutes, until all the water is absorbed and the rice is tender. Meanwhile, hard-boil the eggs and cook the peas. Shell and chop the eggs.

Fork the rice lightly, add 2 of the eggs, the peas and the flaked fish with its juices and butter. Fork together and taste for seasoning.

Bring the cream to the boil in a small pan, season it with salt and plenty of coarsely ground black pepper and add the chopped parsley. Stir just enough into the kedgeree to lightly coat all the ingredients. Garnish just before serving with the remaining chopped egg. Eat hot and serve any remaining cream and parsley sauce separately, as kedgeree can be rather dry.

SALMON KEDGEREE

OILY FISH

IDEAL FOR BARBECUING AND GRILLING, OILY FISH HAVE RICH, MEATY FLESH, USUALLY WITH A FULL FLAVOUR.

ANCHOVY STRONG, PRONOUNCED FLAVOUR. FRESH ANCHOVIES ARE BEST MARINATED, BAKED OR GRILLED, WHILE SMALL FILLETS PACKED IN BRINE OR OIL MAKE EXCELLENT SAUCES (SEE PAGE 41).

HERRING THIS VERSATILE SILVERY FISH WITH A DISTINCTIVE BLUE STREAK ALONG THE BACK LENDS ITSELF TO GRILLING OR FRYING. HERRING ARE CURED TO MAKE INTO BLOATERS, BUCKLING AND KIPPERS.

MACKEREL USUALLY INEXPENSIVE, THIS RICH FISH MUST BE EATEN VERY FRESH AND IS BEST GRILLED. HOT-SMOKED MACKEREL MAKES ALMOST INSTANT PÂTÉS AND MOUSSES.

SALMON THE GROWTH OF SALMON FARMS HAS DONE MUCH TO ALTER THE LUXURY IMAGE OF THIS PALE PINK FISH, ONCE RESERVED FOR SPECIAL OCCASIONS. POACHING IS A GOOD COOKING METHOD BECAUSE IT PREVENTS THE FLESH FROM DRYING OUT BUT SALMON CAN ALSO BE COOKED IN FOIL, GRILLED OR PAN-FRIED. IT TAKES A VERY REFINED PALETTE TO DIFFERENTIATE BETWEEN FARMED AND WILD SALMON, ALTHOUGH THE FARMED FLESH IS OFTEN A BRIGHTER PINK AND MORE OILY AND SUCCULENT WHEN SMOKED.

SALMON TROUT A LARGE SEAGOING TROUT THAT IS EXCELLENT FRIED OR POACHED OR EATEN COLD WITH MAYONNAISE.

SARDINES A GOOD-FLAVOURED SMALLISH FISH, IDEAL FOR COOKING OUTSIDE OVER A FIRE.

TROUT A VERSATILE BUT SOMEWHAT FLAVOURLESS FRESHWATER FISH, BEST BAKED OR FRIED. CAN BE VERY GOOD SMOKED.

TUNA NOT LONG AGO, THIS WAS AN EXPENSIVE LUXURY IN BRITAIN BUT THIS FIRM-FLESHED FISH IS NOW WIDELY AVAILABLE. THE STEAKS ARE IDEAL FOR GRILLING, AND THE FLESH RESPONDS WELL TO MARINATING.

PREPARING HERRING

HERRING ARE OFTEN NICEST WHEN YOU OPEN THEM ALONG THE BACK, LIKE KIPPERS, AND REMOVE THE BACKBONE.

TO DO THIS, FIRST REMOVE THE HEAD AND GUTS IN ONE OPERATION WITHOUT OPENING THE FISH. SIMPLY CUT OFF THE HEAD BEHIND THE GILLS AND PULL OUT THE GUTS IN ONE GO. SCRAPE OFF THE SCALES WITH A BLUNT KNIFE (OR A SCALLOP SHELL, A TRADITIONAL FISH SCALER).

MAKE AN INCISION ALONG THE BACKBONE WITH A SHARP KNIFE, OPEN UP THE FISH SO IT LIES FLAT LIKE AN OPEN BOOK, THEN REMOVE THE BACKBONE, EASING IT OUT CAREFULLY SO YOU TAKE OUT AS MANY OF THE FINE BONES AS POSSIBLE.

HERRING IN OATMEAL

To any Scotsman a meal without oats is a wasted opportunity. This dish of fresh herring coated with oatmeal has a further claim to fame: it was a great favourite of King Edward VII and enjoyed by him not only at Balmoral but when he was living his grand life in London.

Serve these herring with oatcakes and vinegar if you want to be traditional, or with the mustard sauce in the following recipe if you want to follow Edward VII's example, but they are also very delicious simply served with brown bread and butter.

SERVES 4

4 fresh herring, scaled
salt
4 heaped tablespoons medium or fine
oatmeal
lard for frying

*R*emove *the backbone from each herring (see left) and head, if you wish. Pat the fish dry with kitchen paper, and then sprinkle them with salt and coat with oatmeal on both sides, patting it in well.*

Lightly grease a large frying pan with lard, and when it is hot slip in 1 or 2 herring, depending on how much room there is. Fry for 8–10 minutes, until the herring is brown and crisp, turning over several times. Keep warm while you fry the remaining herring.

GRILLED HERRING WITH MUSTARD SAUCE*

It is a good idea to line the grill pan with kitchen foil before using it for fish. Otherwise, rinse it under the tap first with cold water and then with gradually hotter water and lastly in the sink with hot water and bicarbonate of soda to eliminate all trace of fish cooking.

SERVES 4

4 fresh herring
vegetable oil

MUSTARD SAUCE*
1 tablespoon cider vinegar
15 g ($\frac{1}{2}$ oz) butter, softened
1 teaspoon lemon juice
1 teaspoon Dijon mustard
1 teaspoon mustard powder
1 teaspoon brown sugar
1 tablespoon water
1 egg, beaten (*see page 4 for advice on
eggs)
salt and cayenne pepper

*P*reheat the grill to high.
Scale and clean the herrings and wipe them with kitchen paper. Work all the ingredients for the sauce together into a smooth paste in the top of a double boiler or in a heatproof bowl set over a pan of simmering water. Stir gently until the sauce thickens, but do not allow the water to boil. Keep the sauce warm while you grill the herring.

Make 2 or 3 diagonal incisions about 4 cm (1$\frac{1}{2}$ inches) apart on each side of the fish, cutting down to the bone but not through it. Take off the heads and brush the fish with oil. Grill them quickly under the hot grill until brown and crisp on both sides. Serve with the mustard sauce.

MACKEREL PARCELS WITH WATERCRESS SAUCE

This recipe is also suitable for trout.

SERVES 6

6 small very fresh mackerel
60 g (2 oz) butter, melted
salt and freshly ground black pepper
squeeze lemon juice

WATERCRESS SAUCE

15 g (½ oz) butter
15 g (½ oz) plain flour
450 ml (¾ pint) milk
dash dry cider
salt and freshly ground black pepper
2 bunches watercress
hazelnut-sized knob butter

Preheat the oven to 180°C (350°F, Gas 4).

Clean the fish but leave on the heads and tails. Make 2 incisions across the thickest part of the sides to help them cook quickly.

Cut out 6 squares of foil, each large enough to encase a mackerel. Brush the squares of foil with melted butter, put a fish on to each square, season with salt and pepper and a squeeze of lemon juice and fold each one into a little parcel, folding the ends so the juices do not escape. Place on a baking tray and bake for 25 minutes, or 30 minutes for larger fish.

TO MAKE THE WATERCRESS SAUCE

Melt the butter in a saucepan without letting it brown, stir in the flour and when it has foamed up add the milk a little at a time, stirring well after each addition, until you have a smooth sauce. Add the cider and a seasoning of salt and pepper and allow to simmer gently, while you prepare the watercress.

Bring a pan of water to the boil, throw in the watercress, well rinsed and picked over, and let it boil for 2 minutes. Drain it well in a colander, put it on the chopping board and chop it finely. Stir this chopped watercress into the sauce, cover the pan with a tilted lid and let it simmer for a few minutes over a very low heat. Stir in the knob of butter.

To serve, put a parcel on each plate, cut open the top with scissors and let each person unwrap their own fish. Serve watercress sauce separately.

SCENIC FISHING PORT IN DEVON.

GRILLED DOVER SOLE

This recipe is also perfect for other flat fish on the bone, such as lemon sole, large plaice and dabs.

1 Dover sole per person, skinned,
trimmed and cleaned
softened butter
salt and freshly ground black pepper

Heat the grill until it glows before you start to grill the fish. Line the grill pan with buttered kitchen foil.

Spread butter over 1 side of the fish and season with salt and pepper. Grill exactly like a piece of toast, for 4 minutes, until golden brown, then turn the fish over and butter and season the other side. Put them back under the grill for 4 minutes more until golden brown and just cooked through.

Sole vary in thickness and obviously thin ones take less time than thick ones. To test for doneness, look at the head end of the fish and see if it is dry and not pink or red in colour.

Serve very plain with quartered lemons and fried potatoes, or possibly with tartare sauce and small new potatoes.

FLAT-FISH

VERSATILITY IS ONE OF THE ADVANTAGES OF FLAT-FISH FOR THE HOME COOK. THE TENDER FILLETS ARE SUITABLE FOR FRYING, POACHING, STEAMING AND BAKING, WHILE MOST WHOLE FISH STAND UP TO INTENSE HEAT, MAKING THEM IDEAL FOR GRILLING. ANOTHER ADVANTAGE IS THAT THE SIMPLE BONE STRUCTURE MAKES FLAT-FISH EASY TO FILLET IF YOU ARE EVER LUCKY ENOUGH TO BE GIVEN A FRESHLY CAUGHT ONE.

BRILL SOMETIMES UP TO 70 CM (28 INCHES) LONG, THE BRILL'S CREAMY WHITE FLESH IS NOTED FOR ITS FIRM TEXTURE WITH A DELICATE FLAVOUR.

DOVER SOLE WORLD FAMOUS FOR ITS EXCELLENT FLAVOUR AND FIRM TEXTURE. CAN BE COOKED ALL OF THE WAYS ABOVE BUT IT IS BEST SIMPLY GRILLED ON THE BONE, AS IN THE RECIPE RIGHT.

HALIBUT THE LARGEST FLAT-FISH, THIS IS OFTEN SOLD IN STEAKS. COOK QUICKLY OR WITH LIQUID, AS THE FLESH CAN BECOME DRY.

LEMON SOLE NOT REALLY A SOLE; HOWEVER, THIS IS REGARDED AS A POOR RELATION OF THE DOVER SOLE AND, CONSEQUENTLY, IT IS MUCH CHEAPER. THE SWEET FLESH IS EXCELLENT PAN-FRIED OR BAKED IN A SAUCE.

PLAICE AN INEXPENSIVE FISH, GOOD FOR PAN-FRYING AND SERVING WITH CHIPS.

SKATE AN EXCELLENT, INTERESTING FISH WITH A NUTTY FLAVOUR AND LONG-GRAINED FIRM FLESH. BUY SMALLISH SKINNED WINGS AND POACH THEM IN A WELL-FLAVOURED COURT BOUILLON.

TURBOT CONSIDERED THE KING OF FLAT-FISH, TURBOT COMES WITH A PRICE TO REFLECT ITS REGAL REPUTATION. COOK SIMPLY SO THE FLAVOUR IS NOT MASKED.

A DAZZLING DISPLAY OF THE FIRST-CLASS SEAFOOD AND SHELLFISH FROM BRITISH COASTAL WATERS.

TURBOT WITH SHRIMP SAUCE

As far as the British are concerned, the sauce for turbot, brill or halibut – those delicious white-fleshed, thick, flat-fish – needs to be plain. In good traditional kitchens, the simple white or béchamel sauce is beautifully made and has a pure flavour which is enhanced by one simple ingredient. Often it is a humble handful of chopped parsley – Parsley Sauce, for example, is delicious with turbot (see page 155). For a slightly more lavish occasion, it might be button mushroom sauce, oyster sauce, lobster sauce or this shrimp sauce.

SERVES 4

salt
450 ml (¾ pint) milk
4 turbot, brill or halibut steaks, weighing 250 g (8 oz) each

SHRIMP SAUCE

300 ml (½ pint) milk
1 onion
1 bay leaf
8 whole black peppercorns
350 g (12 oz) shrimps or prawns in shells
30 g (1 oz) butter
30 g (1 oz) plain flour
1–2 tablespoons single or double cream

TO MAKE THE SHRIMP SAUCE

*H*eat the milk with the onion, bay leaf and peppercorns, and leave to infuse for 10 minutes. Shell the shrimps or prawns and cook the shells gently in this milk for 10 minutes, then strain the liquid into a bowl, mashing the shells well with the back of a wooden spoon.

Melt the butter in a small saucepan and stir in the flour. Let it cook for 2–3 minutes, then remove from the heat. Add the strained milk gradually to the butter and flour mixture, stirring until it is smooth after each addition.

Let the sauce cook gently for 5–10 minutes, then add 1–2 tablespoons cream and whisk it thoroughly with a fork or stainless steel whisk. When ready to serve, taste for seasoning, add the shellfish and heat through briefly.

COOKING THE FISH

Bring about 2.4 litres (4 pints) well-salted water to the boil, add the milk and when it returns to simmering point turn the heat down until it is barely moving (80°C, 175°F). Slide in the turbot, let it poach very gently for 15–18 minutes, depending on the thickness of the steaks, then remove it to a heated serving dish.

Thin French beans and boiled new potatoes go well with this poached fish. The accompanying shrimp sauce should be very hot.

WEST COUNTRY COD IN BUTTER SAUCE

SERVES 6

½ onion
90 g (3 oz) butter
750 g (1½ lb) cod fillets
salt and freshly ground black pepper
squeeze fresh lemon juice
chopped fresh parsley

*C*hop the half onion finely. Melt 30 g (1 oz) of the butter in a frying pan and soften the onion for 5 minutes, without letting it brown.

Meanwhile, preheat the oven to 180°C (350°F, Gas 4).

Put the fish into a buttered, shallow ovenproof dish. Season it with salt and pepper and spoon the onion and butter mixture over the top. Add the remaining butter and cover the dish with foil. Bake for 20–25 minutes, until the fish flakes easily when the fillets are tested with the tip of a knife.

When the fish is just cooked, spoon the butter and cooking juices into a small pan; keep the fish hot. Add a squeeze of lemon juice and a little chopped parsley to the pan and whisk it over a very gentle heat with a whisk. As you whisk, it will become creamy and opaque. When it is thoroughly whisked pour it over the fish and serve at once.

TURBOT WITH SHRIMP SAUCE (BACK); WEST COUNTRY COD IN BUTTER SAUCE.

TRADITIONAL FISH AND CHIPS

The British and fish and chips have long been inseparable – we even insist on them in the seaports of the Mediterranean, where they do, I believe, have their own ideas about cooking fish. But in spite of the story that they can only be eaten out of newspapers and standing up, they are, in fact, very fine food, particularly when home-made. Fresh haddock is the best fish to use, but you can also use cod or plaice.

SERVES 6

200 g (7 oz) self-raising flour
1 teaspoon salt
½ teaspoon baking powder
3 large haddock fillets, about 300 g
(10 oz) each
vegetable oil for frying
lemon wedges for serving

First get the chips ready (see right), then make the batter. Mix the flour, salt and baking powder and gradually beat in up to 300 ml (½ pint) water to make a thick, rather white batter. Leave to stand for at least 1 hour, then beat again. Skin the haddock fillets and cut them in half.

Heat the vegetable oil in a deep-fat fryer with a basket until it reaches 180–190°C (350–375°F). Dip the pieces of fish first in flour and then in the batter, coating them well but not too thickly.

Deep fry to a crisp golden brown. Drain on kitchen paper. Keep hot in the oven with the door slightly open, while you fry the chips. Serve the fish and chips with lemon wedges.

CHIPS
1.5–1.8 KG (2½–3 LB) POTATOES (MARIS PIPER ARE AMONG THE BEST FOR FRYING)

PEEL THE POTATOES AND CUT INTO CHIPS OF THE SIZE YOU LIKE. IF YOU WANT, YOU CAN CUT THE 2 ROUND ENDS OFF EACH POTATO BEFORE CUTTING THEM, SO YOU HAVE SQUARE-ENDED CHIPS. PUT THEM IN A BOWL OF COLD WATER, AND LEAVE THEM THERE UNTIL JUST BEFORE YOU ARE READY TO START.

DRAIN AND DRY THE CHIPS IN A CLOTH. HEAT THE OIL IN THE DEEP-FRYING PAN TO ABOUT 200°C (400°F).

LOWER THE CHIPS, A FEW AT A TIME, INTO THE HOT FAT AND FRY IN BATCHES, TO A GOLDEN BROWN. DRAIN WELL, LAY OUT ON A BAKING TIN LINED WITH KITCHEN PAPER, SPRINKLE WITH SALT AND KEEP HOT IN THE OVEN WITH THE DOOR VERY SLIGHTLY OPEN, TO PREVENT THEM FROM GOING SOGGY IN THEIR OWN STEAM.

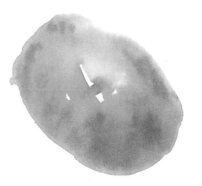

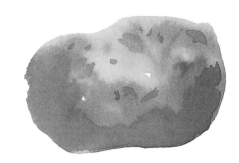

TRADITIONAL FISH AND CHIPS

ROUND FISH

FLAVOURFUL, FIRM FLESH THAT IS NOT TOO BONY AND THRIVES WITH MOST COOKING TECHNIQUES MAKE THESE FISH POPULAR WITH HOME COOKS. HERE ARE A FEW EXAMPLES:

COD SOLD IN FILLETS, STEAKS OR WHOLE, COD IS ONE OF THE MOST POPULAR FISH. ITS SWEET WHITE FLESH MAINTAINS ITS SHAPE, MAKING IT IDEAL FOR KEBABS, FISH AND CHIPS OR BAKING, SEE PAGE 58. TRIMMINGS ARE GOOD FOR MAKING STOCK.

HADDOCK A VERSATILE FISH WITH A FULL FLAVOUR. POPULAR FOR FISH AND CHIPS (SEE PAGE 61), HADDOCK IS ALSO INCLUDED IN MANY FISH PIE RECIPES (SEE RIGHT) AND GOOD FOR GRILLING. WHEN BUYING SMOKED HADDOCK, BE SURE TO LOOK FOR THE NATURAL-COLOURED PALE GOLDEN FLESH RATHER THAN THE DYED BRIGHT YELLOW.

MONKFISH THIS FISH HAS SUCH AN UGLY HEAD THAT IT USED TO BE THE CHEAPEST FISH TO BUY. ONCE PEOPLE OVERLOOKED ITS APPEARANCE AND FOCUSED ON THE RICH, SWEET FLAVOUR ITS POPULARITY INCREASED, AS DID THE PRICE. IDEAL FOR KEBABS AND GRILLING. IT IS VIRTUALLY BONELESS.

RED MULLET VERY SCALY WITH LOTS OF TINY BONES, THIS FISH IS USUALLY PAN-FRIED (SEE RIGHT). SOME OF THE FLAVOUR COMES FROM THE LIVER, WHICH IF NOT LEFT IN THE FISH CAN BE ADDED TO ACCOMPANYING SAUCES.

RED MULLET WITH ANCHOVIES

If you can get fresh red mullet you can cook their livers with the anchovies; they are considered to be a delicacy.

SERVES 4

4 red mullet, about 250 g (8 oz) each,
or 8 small ones, cleaned
15 g (½ oz) butter
1 tablespoon sunflower oil
salt
1 × 50 g tin anchovies in oil
1 lemon, cut in quarters

Scrape the mullet well with the back of a knife to remove all the scales. Rinse the fish well and dry.

Melt the butter with the oil in a frying pan and fry the mullet for 4–5 minutes on each side. Sprinkle with salt, transfer to a heated serving dish and keep hot.

Put the anchovies in the frying pan and fry them until they have almost dissolved. Draw them to one side of the pan, draining off the oil, and put them in 2

A BOUNTIFUL DAY'S CATCH.

mounds, 1 at each end of the dish with the fried mullet.

Give each person a little mound of anchovies, a red mullet and quarter of a lemon. Serve with new potatoes, cooked in their skins, and perhaps some mushrooms sliced, fried in butter and oil and very heavily seasoned with coarse black pepper.

FISH PIE WITH PRAWNS

SERVES 6

750 g (1½ lb) fresh haddock or cod
fillets
500 g (1 lb) Finnan haddock on the
bone, or 350 g (12 oz) smoked haddock
fillets
450 ml (¾ pint) milk
45 g (1½ oz) butter, plus extra for top
of pie
350 g (12 oz) prawns in shells
1 bay leaf
6 whole black peppercorns
45 g (1½ oz) plain flour
salt
¾ teaspoon white wine vinegar
2 tablespoons single or double cream
½ teaspoon freshly ground black pepper,
or more to taste
mashed potatoes made with 750 g
(1½ lb) potatoes, milk and butter

Preheat the oven to 180°C (350°F, Gas 4). Put the fillets of fish and Finnan haddock in an ovenproof dish with the milk. Dot with 15 g (½ oz) butter and bake for 20 minutes. When cool enough to handle, skin the fish, remove the bones and set the flesh aside.

Shell the prawns (reserving the shells), and add them to the fish.

Heat the milk in which the fish was cooked, together with the prawn shells, bay leaf and peppercorns. Let it infuse over a very low heat for at least 10

minutes. Increase the oven temperature to 200°C (400°F, Gas 6).

Melt the remaining 30 g (1 oz) butter in a medium-sized pan, stir in the flour and let it cook for 1 minute. Then remove from the heat and stir in the strained milk. Make a nice thick, smooth sauce, then season it carefully with salt, wine vinegar, cream and masses of black pepper. The flavour of this sauce is most important and must not be bland.

Stir in the fish and prawns and transfer the mixture to a 25 cm (10 inch) oval pie dish. Cover with well-seasoned mashed potato, dot with butter and bake in the oven until the top is nicely browned. Serve very hot.

SCALLOPS WITH FRIED BREADCRUMBS

SERVES 4

12 fresh scallops
30 g (1 oz) butter
4 tablespoons olive oil
45 g (½ oz) fresh white breadcrumbs
salt and freshly ground black pepper
1 lemon, quartered

*C*lean and wash the scallops and put them to drain and dry in a colander.

Heat half the butter and oil in a small frying pan and fry the breadcrumbs, moving them about all the time to prevent

TRADITIONAL SCOTTISH HERRING SMOKING.

them burning, until they are a good even brown and quite crisp.

Heat the remaining oil and butter in a second pan. When it is very hot, put in the scallops, then turn down the heat a little and let them cook and glaze to a glossy brown over a moderate heat for about 2 minutes on each side – but make sure they keep frying and don't start cooking in their own juices.

Season with salt and pepper, throw the breadcrumbs over the scallops and cook for 30 seconds more. Serve at once, well sprinkled with the crumbs, with a quarter of a lemon on each plate.

POULTRY AND GAME

S o much depends on the quality of poultry, particularly today; the difference between a chicken, turkey or duck reared in the now outdated intensive manner, and one that has enjoyed space, exercise and fresh air, is quite remarkable. In some ways the intensive bird scores points, because it is tender, moist and has plentiful meat on it. However, it tends to be wet rather than juicy, and the flavour is generally pretty dull. The skin is often thin and does not crisp well, and there is something slightly bland about the whole thing. An outdoor bird can be less tender, it may even be less moist, but it scores in having wonderful concentrated juices and a rich and interesting flavour, and the skin will become good and crisp when roasted.

The quality of game is less predictable, but it is worth the slight gamble; pheasants are particularly good value now. I always buy farmed rabbit and pigeon, which guarantees tenderness.

DUCK WITH GLAZED YOUNG TURNIPS (PAGE 71)

POULTRY GUIDE

CHICKENS:

BOILERS NOT USUALLY SOLD IN SUPER-MARKETS, THESE ARE OLD BIRDS WEIGHING UP TO ABOUT 3.5 KG (7 LB). AS THE NAME IMPLIES, THESE ARE BEST SUITED TO LONG COOKING IN A LARGE POT OF WATER. DO NOT TAKE THE NAME TOO LITERALLY, HOWEVER, AS THEY SHOULD BE GENTLY SIMMERED, NOT BOILED. ALSO GOOD CASSEROLED.

ROASTERS THE VAST MAJORITY OF BIRDS FALL INTO THIS CATEGORY, WEIGHING 1.2–2 KG (2½–4 LB) AND SERVING 3 TO 4 PEOPLE. THEY ARE SOLD WHOLE OR JOINTED AND FRESH OR FROZEN, ALTHOUGH MOST BIRDS FROM SUPERMARKETS ARE, IN FACT, CHILLED. ROASTING, GRILLING AND POACHING ARE ALL SUITABLE COOKING METHODS. BE SURE TO SAVE THE CARCASES FOR MAKING STOCK (SEE PAGE 20).

CORN-FED EASILY DISTINGUISHED BY THEIR PALE YELLOW SKIN, THESE BIRDS HAVE BETTER FLAVOURED FLESH THAN STANDARD TABLE CHICKENS. GOOD FOR ROASTING, POACHING AND GRILLING.

FREE-RANGE ALTHOUGH ALL BIRDS LABELLED 'FREE-RANGE' HAVE TO BE GIVEN ACCESS TO OPEN SPACE AND LEFT TO MOVE AROUND AT WILL FOR AT LEAST 28 DAYS, IT IS A MISTAKE TO IMAGINE OLD-FASHIONED FAR-MYARD SCENES. ONLY THOSE SPECIFICALLY LABELLED 'FREE-RANGE TOTAL FREEDOM' HAVE NOT BEEN RAISED WITH THOUSANDS OF OTHER BIRDS IN LARGE BARNS LEFT OPEN AT BOTH ENDS.

POUSSINS IDEAL FOR INDIVIDUAL SERVINGS, THESE SMALL BIRDS ARE BUTCHERED AT 4–6 WEEKS AND DO NOT WEIGH MORE THAN 625 G (1¼ LB).

DUCKS THIS FATTY BIRD IS BEST ROASTED SO THE FAT DRAINS OFF DURING COOKING.

GOOSE OFTEN FORGOTTEN EX-CEPT AT CHRISTMAS, THIS DELICIOUS BIRD IS ALSO VERY FATTY AND BEST SUITED TO ROASTING.

GUINEA FOWL ONCE WILD, THIS BIRD HAS BEEN DOMESTICATED AND IS NOW AVAILABLE ALL YEAR ROUND. ITS FLESH IS SIMILAR TO CHICKEN BUT THE FLAVOUR IS GAMIER.

TO ROAST A CHICKEN – A FAMILY RECIPE

This is a traditional, plain, golden roast bird with a light stuffing, very much nicer and more delicate than a dense solid one. You can add grated lemon rind and chopped parsley and thyme or fresh tarragon to the stuffing if you like, and also the chopped chicken liver, fried with a little chopped onion. Use the neck, gizzard and heart to make the stock (see page 20).

SERVES 4

1 roasting chicken, weighing 1.5 kg
(3 lb), free-range if possible
2–3 tablespoons fresh brown or white
breadcrumbs
1 tablespoon chopped fresh parsley and
½–1 teaspoon fresh or dried thyme
salt and freshly ground black pepper
75 g (2½ oz) butter
plain flour for dusting

GRAVY

3–4 tablespoons chicken stock,
preferably home-made (see page 20)
2–3 tablespoons double cream
2 teaspoons dry sherry

*P*reheat the oven to 190°C (375°F, Gas 5). Remove any rubber bands or giblets in plastic bags from your chicken, as they will not improve the flavour. Fill the cavity with breadcrumbs mixed with chopped parsley and thyme and seasoned with salt and plenty of pepper. Add 30 g (1 oz) butter, then truss the legs with string.

Put the chicken into a roasting tin, cover the breast with flakes of butter, a sprinkling of thyme and a piece of buttered greaseproof paper. Put the remaining butter in the tin. Roast, lifting the paper to baste the bird once or twice.

After 1 hour remove the paper, dust the bird with flour and baste with juices from the roasting tin. Return to the oven, uncovered, for 15 minutes to crisp and brown.

Meanwhile, make a little concentrated stock by reducing some stock with the chicken giblets to make 3–4 tablespoons. (Make sure you trim off any greenish patches on the liver, as they taste bitter.)

TO MAKE THE GRAVY

Test the bird by pricking the thick part of the leg with a needle or skewer. If the juices run clear, the bird is cooked. Remove the chicken from the roasting tin and keep hot while you add the stock to the juices in the tin. Boil for 2–3 minutes, scraping up the juices. Then stir in the cream and sherry and boil until it reaches a good consistency. Remember when you are carving to give each person a spoonful of the breadcrumbs from inside the bird – they are delicious.

CHICKEN PIE

I find, happily, we can all be cheerful and merry with nothing but this chicken pie for the main course. Cream, parsley and coarsely crushed white pepper make a delicious sauce. A cold version is made by leaving out the flour and butter from the sauce; the stock with its cream sets to a nice creamy jelly when cold.

SERVES 6

1 roasting chicken, weighing about
1.7 kg (3½ lb)
2 sticks celery
1 onion
2 leeks
1 bunch fresh herbs – parsley, thyme
and bay leaf
3 tablespoons dry white wine
salt
30 g (1 oz) butter
30 g (1 oz) plain flour
1 teaspoon coarsely crushed *white*
peppercorns
150 ml (¼ pint) double cream
3 tablespoons chopped fresh parsley
Rough Puff Pastry made with 180 g
(6 oz) flour (see page 187)
1 egg, beaten, for glazing

*P*ut the chicken into a saucepan which fits it fairly closely. Cover it with water and bring it to the boil. Lower the heat to a simmer, skimming well. Then add the celery, onion, leeks, herbs, wine and seasoning and simmer steadily for 1 hour.

Lift out the chicken, strain the stock and return it to the pan to reduce by boiling to 300 ml (½ pint).

Remove the chicken from the bones and put the pieces into a 25 cm (10 inch) pie dish with a pie funnel in the middle.

Make a sauce with the butter, flour, stock from the chicken and the coarsely crushed white peppercorns. This is important for the eventual flavour of the pie.

Add the cream and at least 3 tablespoons chopped parsley. Pour it over the chicken and fold it in so that all the chicken is coated with it. Leave to cool.

Preheat the oven to 220°C (425°F, Gas 7). Cover the pie with a crust (see the recipe for Steak and Kidney Pie, page 92), glaze and bake in the oven for 10 minutes. Then lower the oven temperature to 180°C (350°F, Gas 4) and bake for a further 20 minutes or more; at this moderate heat it will not spoil if it has to wait until you are ready for it.

MAKING BUNCHES OF HERBS

A CLASSIC WAY OF FLAVOURING DISHES DURING COOKING IS TO ADD A BOUQUET OF FRESH HERBS, AS IN THE CHICKEN PIE RECIPE LEFT. YOU CAN BUY PREPARED SACHETS OF DRIED HERBS BUT I PREFER TO USE FRESH HERBS. SIMPLY TIE A FEW SPRIGS OR LEAVES OF YOUR CHOSEN HERBS TOGETHER WITH A PIECE OF STRING. IF YOU MAKE THE STRING LONG ENOUGH IT CAN BE TIED TO THE PAN'S HANDLE FOR EASY REMOVAL AT THE END OF COOKING. DON'T FORGET TO BRUISE STEMS LIGHTLY TO RELEASE EXTRA FLAVOUR. IF YOU WANT TO RELEASE THE HERB FLAVOUR BUT YOU DO NOT WISH THE LEAVES TO MIX IN WITH THE OTHER INGREDIENTS, WRAP THEM IN A PIECE OF LEEK AND TIE WITH STRING.

KENTISH CHICKEN PUDDING

This pudding would originally have been boiled in a cloth but is lighter and, I think, better made in a pudding basin like a steak and kidney pudding. It can be made with a boiling or roasting bird.

SERVES 4–6

1 chicken, weighing 1.7–2 kg (3½–4 lb)
125 g (4 oz) button mushrooms
2 thick slices cooked ham, about
60 g (2 oz)
1 tablespoon chopped fresh parsley
30 g (1 oz) seasoned flour
salt and freshly ground black pepper
300 ml (½ pint) chicken stock,
preferably home-made (see page 20)

SUET CRUST
250 g (8 oz) self-raising flour
125 g (4 oz) grated suet
salt and freshly ground black pepper
water, to mix

Joint the chicken. Place chicken breast side up. Pull the leg away from the body and use a sharp knife to cut down to the ball and socket joint. Use the knife's tip to free the flesh around the joint, then pull down to free the joint and cut the leg off. You can then cut the leg joint into a drumstick and thigh or leave whole, depending how many pieces you want. Repeat with the other leg.

Cut off the wing by cutting from the breast towards the wing joint. Repeat on the other side and cut off both wing tips. To separate breast meat from the rib cage and the carcase, cut along the natural break. You can then cut off the breast. Place the breast skin side down and cut along the centre to make 2 pieces. Be sure to save the bones for making stock (see page 20). Take the meat off the bone and cut into neat pieces. Clean the mushrooms and chop coarsely, together with the ham and parsley. Roll the pieces of chicken in seasoned flour.

Make the suet crust by mixing flour, suet and salt and pepper in a bowl. Add enough water to make a soft but not sticky dough. Cover and leave to rest for 10–15 minutes.

Take two-thirds of the dough and roll it out on a floured surface. Use it to line a greased 1.5 litre (2½ pint) pudding basin. Fill the basin with layers of chicken pieces, season and sprinkle with the chopped mushrooms and ham mixture.

Pour in the stock. Brush the top edge of the crust with water, and place the remaining crust, rolled out into a disc, on top. Press the edges together well, trim and cover the top with a loose lid of foil (to allow for rising) tied on with string. Make a handle of string for lifting the pudding out of the pan.

Place it in a large saucepan half full of boiling water, cover and boil for 3 hours, topping up the pan with more boiling water if necessary.

When the cooking time is up, lift the pudding out of the pan and remove the foil. Wrap the basin in a white napkin and serve the pudding straight from the bowl.

Kentish Chicken Pudding (left); Steak and Kidney Pudding (page 92)

FREE-RANGE CHICKENS ROAMING AROUND
THE FARMYARD.

GRILLED CHICKEN WITH A SHARP SAUCE

Nathaniel Gubbins, sporting author and a great gourmet at the turn of the century, invented many piquant dishes, of which I think this is best.

SERVES 4

8 chicken drumsticks
vegetable oil
salt and freshly ground black pepper

GUBBINS SAUCE
60 g (2 oz) butter
3 tablespoons freshly made English mustard
3 dessertspoons tarragon vinegar
4 tablespoons double cream
salt and freshly ground black pepper

*M*ake the sauce in the top of a double boiler or in a heatproof bowl set over a pan of gently simmering water. The water should be low enough not to touch the base of the top pan or bowl. Melt the butter, stir in the mustard, the vinegar and lastly the cream. Season with salt and pepper, and keep the sauce hot, over simmering water, while you grill the chicken pieces.

Preheat the grill to high.

Brush the chicken drumsticks with oil, season them with salt and pepper and cover the ends of the leg bones with kitchen foil.

Now grill under the hot grill for 20 minutes, turning the drumsticks from time to time.

Test by piercing with a skewer at the fattest part of the leg; if a colourless bead of liquid falls, it is done, if rose-red, it needs a little longer. When the drumsticks are cooked through serve them immediately with the sauce poured over.

JOSEFA'S CHICKEN CURRY

SERVES 4

1 roasting chicken, weighing about
1.5 kg (3 lb)
2 onions
4 cm (1½ inch) piece fresh root ginger,
peeled
2–3 small green chillies, seeded
3 large cloves garlic
3 tablespoons vegetable oil
3 tablespoons curry powder
450 ml (¾ pint) milk, or coconut milk
salt and freshly ground black pepper
1–2 teaspoons chutney (Orange
Chutney, page 162, is good)
boiled rice for serving

SIDE DISHES

2 eggs, hard-boiled and chopped
2 tomatoes, skinned and chopped
60–90 g (2–3 oz) roasted peanuts or
cashew nuts
½ onion, chopped
2 bananas, sliced

*C*ut the chicken into 8 neat pieces.
Chop the onions, ginger, chillies and
garlic finely. (Take care to wash your
hands after handling chillies.)

Heat the oil in a flameproof casserole
and fry the chicken until pale golden on
all sides. Remove the pieces. Lower the
heat and fry the onions, garlic, chillies,
ginger and curry powder until the onions
are soft. Return the chicken to the casserole and pour on the milk. Add salt, pepper
and chutney and simmer fairly rapidly for
40 minutes, until the chicken is cooked
through.

Put the ingredients for the side dishes
separately into little bowls. Serve the curry
with plenty of rice and the side dishes.

DUCK WITH GLAZED YOUNG TURNIPS

This is a very ancient combination of
flavours. The Romans served both duck
and crane with turnips and in Eliza-
bethan times older birds were often
boiled with turnips. Today, we prefer to
eat young crisp-skinned roast duck with
young turnips glazed to a beautiful
bronze in sugar and butter.

SERVES 3–4

1 duck, weighing 2.2 kg (4½ lb)
salt and freshly ground black pepper
1 bunch fresh herbs – parsley, thyme
and marjoram
1 shallot or small onion
1 large glass dry white wine
12 small young turnips
1 dessertspoon sugar

*P*reheat the oven to 200°C (400°F,
Gas 6).

Put the duck, salted inside and out, in
the roasting tin. Slip the herbs inside it
and place the sliced shallot in the pan
with the duck. Pour in the glass of white
wine and put the duck in the oven for
1¼–1½ hours. Every now and then baste
the duck with the wine and prick its skin
here and there with a fork or cocktail stick
to allow the fat to escape during roasting.
It will become deliciously crisp.

In the meantime, cook the giblets in
600 ml (1 pint) water, letting it simmer
and reduce for 1 hour, to obtain 300 ml
(½ pint) reduced stock.

While the duck is roasting, peel the
turnips carefully and put them in a pan of
cold salted water. Bring to the boil, then
simmer for 15–20 minutes, until just
tender. Drain the turnips and return them
to the pan together with the melted butter
and the sugar. Cook them in this glaze for
15 minutes until they are nicely bronzed
and shiny, give them a shake from time to
time, to brown them evenly.

When the duck is cooked, remove it to
a hot serving dish, place the turnips round
and keep it hot.

Spoon off all the fat from the juices in
the roasting tin. Bring the juices to the
boil, stir in the strained giblet stock and
let it simmer for 5 minutes, scraping up
the juices from round the tin with a
wooden spoon. Taste for seasoning, and
add further salt and pepper if necessary.
Strain into a sauceboat and serve separately, piping hot.

TURKEY WITH PRUNES

Make the stock for the gravy the day before so you can take off all the fat. When it has been in the refrigerator the fat sets on top in a layer that you can just lift off with a spoon.

SERVES 10–12

24 prunes
cold, strained tea
2–3 tablespoons port or sherry
125 g (4 oz) smoked streaky bacon in 1 piece, rind removed if necessary
7.5 kg (15 lb) turkey, all feather stubs removed
60 g (2 oz) good-quality walnut halves, or better still freshly shelled walnuts
salt and freshly ground black pepper
125 g (4 oz) butter
30 small onions, about 1 kg (2 lb), preferably silver onions
4 teaspoons icing sugar

A SELECTION OF HORSE CHESTNUTS.

CHESTNUT STUFFING

YOU CAN ALSO STUFF THE NECK END OF THE TURKEY WITH A CONVENTIONAL CHESTNUT AND SAUSAGEMEAT STUFFING.

TO MAKE THIS, BUY 500 G (1 LB) OF THE BEST SAUSAGES YOU CAN FIND, SKIN THEM AND PUT THE SAUSAGEMEAT INTO A BOWL. ADD 1 EGG, 10 BOILED, SHELLED AND PEELED CHESTNUTS (SEE PAGE 77), 2 CHOPPED SHALLOTS FRIED IN BUTTER, AND SEASONINGS OF PEPPER, SALT, NUTMEG AND CHOPPED FRESH PARSLEY. FRY A LITTLE OF THIS TO CHECK THE SEASONING, AND THEN USE IT TO STUFF THE NECK END OF THE TURKEY UNDER THE SKIN. USE A SKEWER TO FASTEN THE NATURAL POCKET MADE BY THE FLAP, SO IT DOES NOT COME UNDONE DURING ROASTING.

FOR THE STOCK
turkey giblets
125 g (4 oz) stewing beef
2 chicken wings or 2 sets of chicken giblets
1 large onion stuck with 1 clove
1 bay leaf
12 whole black peppercorns
a little salt

FOR THE GRAVY
150 ml (¼ pint) dry red wine or sherry
1 teaspoon potato flour
salt and freshly ground pepper
knob butter

THE DAY BEFORE

Put all the stock ingredients in a large pan with plenty of cold water. Bring to the boil and skim off the scum, then simmer very, very slowly for about 2 hours, uncovered, to keep clear. Strain, leaving all sediment behind, cool and then refrigerate. If it seems weak, strengthen the flavour by simmering to reduce the quantity.

Soak the prunes overnight in a little tea and 2–3 tablespoons port or sherry.

ON THE DAY

Preheat the oven to 180°C (350°F, Gas 4). Drain the prunes. Cut the bacon into sticks and blanch in boiling water for 2–3 minutes; drain well, then brown lightly in its own fat in a small frying pan.

Fill the turkey with prunes, walnuts and bacon, season lightly and sew or skewer the opening and, if necessary, truss the legs together with string. Put in the roasting tin with 4 tablespoons water and cover the breast and legs with 60 g (2 oz) butter cut in flakes.

Roast for 3¼–3½ hours, turning and basting it every 30 minutes. When it is a beautiful, even brown, cover with buttered greaseproof paper (not foil) and finish

roasting, until the juices run clear when the thickest point of the thigh is pierced.

GLAZED ONIONS

Meanwhile, peel the onions and put in a wide pan in a single layer. Add 60 g (2 oz) butter, the sugar, 150 ml ($\frac{1}{4}$ pint) water and a pinch of salt.

Cook, stirring frequently with a wooden spoon, until the water has evaporated and the onions are coated with a brown syrupy glaze. Keep aside in this pan ready to reheat.

THE GRAVY

When the turkey is cooked, remove it from the roasting tin to its serving platter.

Remove most of the fat from the tin, then add the wine or sherry and several generous ladles of stock. Blend the potato flour with 1–2 tablespoons cold water. Stir it into the gravy and bring to the boil, stirring constantly and scraping the tin well. Cook for 5 minutes, adding more stock as necessary. The gravy should be glossy, dark brown and rich. Reduce if necessary, then season well and you can stir in a knob of butter at this point.

TO SERVE

Remove the skewers or string from the turkey and carefully take out the prunes, bacon and walnuts with a large spoon. Pile them, mixed with the hot glazed onions, round the front of the turkey on its serving platter.

Serve with roast potatoes, Brussels sprouts with fried breadcrumbs (75 g/3 oz fresh breadcrumbs fried in 60 g/2 oz butter), the gravy and cranberry jelly.

AN IDYLLIC FARMYARD SCENE WITH GRAZING POULTRY.

ROAST GOOSE WITH APPLE SAUCE

Traditionally, geese are eaten at Michaelmas on 29 October, having just been fattened on the gleaning from the wheat and barley. As goose is served so seldom it would be a pity not to do it properly in the old way with a home-made sage and onion stuffing.

SERVES 6

1 goose, weighing 6 kg (12 lb)
salt
1 glass dry white wine
600 ml (1 pint) stock made with goose giblets (see page 20)
1½ tablespoons plain flour

SAGE AND ONION STUFFING

salt
4 large onions
30 g (1 oz) butter
125 g (4 oz) fresh breadcrumbs
salt and freshly ground black pepper
20 fresh sage leaves, chopped, or 1 dessertspoon dried sage
1 egg beaten with 1 teaspoon milk

APPLE SAUCE

1 kg (2 lb) cooking apples
15 g (½ oz) butter
2 teaspoons sugar

*T*o make the stuffing, bring a pan of salted water to the boil and boil the skinned onions for 30 minutes, until they are tender. Strain, cool and chop the onions, then cook them in the butter for 10 minutes. Now leave them to cool, then mix them with the remaining stuffing ingredients in a bowl.

Preheat the oven to 220°C (425°F, Gas 7). Salt the goose inside and out, picking off any stray quills. Fill the cavity with the stuffing and put the goose on a rack in a large roasting tin. Prick the skin here and there with a fork so fat which lies under the skin melts out during roasting.

Pour the glass of dry white wine and 600 ml (1 pint) water into the roasting tin and roast for 1 hour, basting with the liquid from time to time. Turn down the heat to 190°C (375°F, Gas 5) and roast for a further 1½ hours, continuing to baste. Cover with foil for the last hour.

When the goose is cooked through, remove to a large serving platter and put it back in the oven which can now be turned off. The meat will settle, making it easier to carve.

Meanwhile, spoon out most of the fat from the roasting tin. Add 1½ tablespoons flour to the gravy left in the tin, stirring it round until it has cooked and thickened.

Taste the gravy for seasoning and add boiling goose giblet stock if it is too con-centrated. Strain the gravy it into a gravy boat and serve the goose with this sauce and the sage and onion stuffing as well as the apple sauce.

TO MAKE THE APPLE SAUCE

While the goose is roasting, peel and core the apples. Put them over a low heat in a covered pan with very little water. When they are soft and fluffy beat them with a fork, adding the butter and sugar to taste (this rather varies according to the tart-ness of the apples, but do not make the sauce too sweet). Serve the apple sauce very hot.

ROAST PHEASANT WITH APPLES

This recipe, which is best made in the autumn with a young pheasant and windfall apples, can be used equally well for an old pheasant by lengthening the cooking time to $1\frac{1}{2}$ hours.

SERVES 4

90 g (3 oz) butter, or 3 tablespoons vegetable oil and 30 g (1 oz) butter
1 young pheasant
6 cooking apples
1 tablespoon sugar
1 bay leaf
salt and freshly ground black pepper
4 tablespoons single cream
30 g (1 oz) fresh breadcrumbs fried in 30 g (1 oz) butter
1 bunch watercress

*H*eat 90 g (3 oz) butter, or the oil together with 30 g (1 oz) butter, in a flameproof casserole and brown the pheasant on all sides.

Meanwhile, preheat the oven to 180°C (350°F, Gas 4). Peel and core the apples and cut them into slices. Transfer the pheasant to a dish and put the sliced apples into the casserole, sprinkle them with the sugar and let them cook gently until they start to soften. Place the bird on top and add the bay leaf and seasoning. Cover and cook for 45 minutes.

Now pour in the cream, mix it into the apples. Serve the pheasant resting in its apple bed, which can be sprinkled with golden fried breadcrumbs, and which serves as sauce and gravy.

Place a small bunch of watercress on each plate and accompany the dish with a fresh vegetable such as Savoy cabbage.

AN OLD-FASHIONED, TRADITIONAL VILLAGE SHOP WITH A SELECTION OF FRESH GAME.

BRAISED GUINEA FOWL WITH CHESTNUTS

SERVES 4

1 guinea fowl, weighing 1.5 kg (2½ lb),
cleaned but with liver and heart
reserved
30–60 g (1–2 oz) streaky bacon, rind
removed if necessary
250 g (8 oz) button onions
250 g (8 oz) carrots
250 g (8 oz) chestnuts
30 g (1 oz) butter
1 tablespoon vegetable oil
1 bunch fresh herbs – parsley, thyme
and bay leaf
salt and freshly ground black pepper
2–3 tablespoons red wine
150 ml (¼ pint) chicken stock,
preferably home-made (see page 20)

Preheat the oven to 180°C (350°F, Gas 4).

Joint the guinea fowl, and cut the bacon into pieces. Peel the onions and carrots and peel the chestnuts.

Heat the butter and oil in a flameproof casserole. Fry the bacon and pieces of guinea fowl, browning them nicely on both sides, then remove them to a bowl. Now fry the vegetables with the guinea fowl liver and heart, cut in pieces, browning them lightly.

When they look appetizing, return the bacon, add the chestnuts and put the pieces of guinea fowl back on top. Push the bunch of herbs into the centre, season and add the wine and stock.

Cover the casserole and cook in the oven for 45 minutes. Serve with mashed potatoes.

TO PEEL CHESTNUTS

Make a cut on the flat side with a small knife, then drop the chestnuts into a pan of boiling, salted water and boil for 1–2 minutes. Remove 2 or 3 at a time with a slotted spoon because they should be peeled hot, then peel away both shells and the bitter inner skins. Time and patience are needed to this job properly.

BRAISED PIGEONS WITH GREEN PEAS

This is based on a nineteenth-century recipe from the Red Lion Hotel, Fareham, in Hampshire.

SERVES 4

3 rashers bacon, rinds removed if
necessary, and cut up small
45 g (1½ oz) butter
125 g (4 oz) mushrooms
4 pigeons, preferably young
a little plain flour
1 onion, chopped
150 ml (¼ pint) dry red wine
1 bunch fresh herbs – basil, thyme,
marjoram and parsley
freshly grated nutmeg
ground allspice
lemon rind, pared free of white pith
squeeze lemon juice
salt and freshly ground black pepper
350 g (12 oz) shelled peas

Preheat the oven to 170°C (325°F, Gas 3).

In a heavy-based flameproof casserole, fry the bacon in 30 g (1 oz) butter, then after 1–2 minutes add the mushrooms. When they are lightly cooked, take them out. Dust the pigeons with flour, add a little more butter to the casserole and brown the pigeons all over. When they are seared, remove them and fry the onion until tender but not brown.

Stir the mushrooms and bacon back into the pan, put the pigeons on top and pour on the red wine. Add the herbs, a pinch each of nutmeg and allspice, the lemon rind and juice and salt and pepper. Bring to simmering point, cover the casserole and braise until tender. If they are young 45 minutes–1 hour should be enough, but older pigeons will need longer.

Meanwhile, cook the peas in rapidly boiling well-salted water. Drain well and set aside.

When the pigeons are done, remove them with a slotted spoon and arrange in an oval gratin dish. Arrange the bacon and mushrooms around and over the tops. Skim the fat from the juices and reheat the peas in the juices. Serve the pigeons with the skimmed gravy, bacon, mushrooms and peas.

BRAISED GUINEA FOWL WITH CHESTNUTS

PARTRIDGE WITH CABBAGE

SERVES 4

250 g (8 oz) streaky bacon, rind
removed if necessary
1 tablespoon vegetable oil
4 partridges or pigeons
4 small onions, quartered
1 green cabbage, cut into eighths
12 whole black peppercorns
3 bay leaves
2 tablespoons wine vinegar
300 ml ($\frac{1}{2}$ pint) chicken stock,
preferably home-made (see page 20)
150 ml ($\frac{1}{4}$ pint) port
salt and freshly ground black pepper
knob butter
1 dessertspoon plain flour

*P*reheat the oven to 170°C (325°F,
Gas 3).

Cut the bacon into 2.5 cm (1 inch)
cubes. Put the bacon in the bottom of a
casserole with the oil and let it render
some of its fat over a gentle heat. Brown

the partridges all over in this and remove
them to a dish. Now add the onions and
the cabbage and let them soften a little in
the bacon fat. Add the pepper, bay leaves,
vinegar, stock and port, a very little salt
and plenty of freshly ground pepper.

Season the partridges and return them
to the casserole, cover with a sheet of
kitchen foil and then a well-fitting lid and
cook for 1$\frac{1}{2}$ hours.

Remove the birds and place the onions
and cabbage round them with a slotted
spoon. Skim the fat from the liquid, then
strain it and thicken it with a knob of
butter the size of a walnut mashed to a
paste with 1 dessertspoon flour. Let it boil
over a moderate heat while you drop in
pieces of the paste. When the sauce has
thickened, cook it for 2–3 minutes more,
then taste for seasoning, and pour it over
the birds and vegetables.

ROAST GROUSE WITH LETTUCE HEARTS

Grouse come into season in August, a
happy moment for lovers of game. For
this recipe you must have the tight-
hearted crisp little lettuces called Little
Gem or Buttercrunch, or small Cos
lettuces.

SERVES 4

4 young grouse
sprinkling plain flour
125 g (4 oz) butter
salt and freshly ground black pepper
4 rashers bacon, rinds removed if
necessary, pounded thin and cut in half
crossways
150 ml ($\frac{1}{4}$ pint) dry red wine
150 ml ($\frac{1}{4}$ pint) game or chicken stock,
preferably home-made (see page 20)
3–4 lettuce heads (see above), all
outside leaves removed

*P*reheat the oven to 220°C (425°F,
Gas 7).

Dust the grouse with flour, put a little
nut of butter and a sprinkling of salt and
pepper inside each one. Fry the birds in
the remaining butter in a small roasting
tin until they are sealed and golden brown
all over, then cover the breasts with
rashers of bacon.

Place the roasting tin with the grouse
in the hot oven. After 8–10 minutes baste
them, lower the oven temperature to
180°C (350°F, Gas 4) and cook for a
further 15 minutes. Keep the grouse hot
on a serving platter, surrounded with the
bacon.

Skim the fat off the juices in the roasting tin, add the wine and boil, uncovered,
to reduce to 2–3 tablespoons. Then add
the stock and reduce again until the flavour is rich enough for your taste. Taste
for seasoning and put into a hot gravy
boat.

Quarter the lettuce hearts and serve
each person with a grouse, a piece of
bacon and 3 or 4 quarters of lettuce heart
with the roasting juices poured over. The
combination of the hot gravy and hearts
of lettuce is quite delicious.

ROAST GROUSE WITH LETTUCE HEARTS WITH
GAME CHIPS (PAGE 122)

RABBIT PIE

Rabbit pie has an excellent flavour and is very much enjoyed in the British countryside where rabbits are still all too plentiful.

SERVES 4–6

1 large rabbit, preferably farmed
a little plain flour
1 tablespoon butter or lard
1–2 tablespoons vegetable oil
250 g (8 oz) onions, coarsely chopped
125 g (4 oz) streaky bacon, rind removed if necessary, cut in pieces
¼–½ teaspoon each dried marjoram, lemon thyme and savory
1 bay leaf
1 strip lemon rind, chopped (pare the yellow zest carefully avoiding the bitter white pith)
300 ml (½ pint) beef stock, preferably home-made (see page 20)
generous dash port or dry red wine
salt and freshly ground black pepper
4–5 slender carrots
1 lump sugar
butter
250 g (8 oz) shortcrust pastry
1 egg yolk, beaten, for glazing

*C*ut the rabbit into serving-size pieces and dust them freely in flour. Fry them, a few at a time, in the 1–2 tablespoons butter or lard and oil, in a flameproof casserole with a heavy base. When they are a rich golden brown, fry the onions and the bacon in the same fat over a low heat. Return the pieces of rabbit.

Add the herbs, lemon rind, stock, port or wine and seasoning. Cover and simmer gently for 45 minutes–1 hour for a farm-bred rabbit – a wild one may take longer,

RABBIT PIE WITH MASHED POTATOES AND SPRING ONIONS (PAGE 122)

according to its age.

If there seems to be too much gravy when the rabbit is tender, pour it into a small pan and simmer it, uncovered, until it is somewhat reduced. Taste for seasoning and leave to cool.

Clean the carrots, slice them about the thickness of a 1p piece and blanch for 5 minutes in boiling water with salt, a lump of sugar and a nut of butter. Drain them and set them aside.

Preheat the oven to 200°C (400°F, Gas 6).

Transfer the rabbit and its juices to a large pie dish and scatter the carrots over the top. Cover with rolled out pastry, using a double thickness for the rim and taking care that it does not get stretched or it will shrink in the oven. Decorate the top with pastry leaves or rabbits and brush with egg yolk beaten with salt and a little water. Scallop or fork the edges of the pie, glaze a second time and bake for 15 minutes, then cover the pie loosely with foil, lower the heat to 180°C (350°F, Gas 4) and bake for a further 25 minutes.

Serve with Mashed Potatoes with Spring Onions (see page 122).

ALTERNATIVE

Instead of carrots you can scatter over the top of the cooked rabbit a quantity of thinly sliced mushrooms cooked for 1–2 minutes in butter.

JUGGED HARE

As with most game, hare needs to have a little sweetness added during cooking, which is the redcurrant jelly in this recipe.

SERVES 4

1 hare, jointed, with its blood reserved
30 g (1 oz) seasoned flour
60 g (2 oz) butter
2 tablespoons vegetable oil
125 g (4 oz) streaky bacon, rind removed if necessary
4 carrots
2 onions
2 glasses dry red wine
good pinch each ground cloves and cinnamon
good pinch grated nutmeg
salt and freshly ground black pepper
300 ml (½ pint) chicken stock, preferably home-made (see page 20)
15 g (½ oz) butter
1 tablespoon plain flour
1 teaspoon redcurrant jelly

*R*oll the hare joints in plenty of sea-soned flour. Heat the butter and oil in a large flameproof casserole and fry the joints to a rich mahogany-brown all over. Transfer them to a large plate and then throw the bacon into the casserole, cut into pieces about 2.5 cm (1 inch) square, the carrots cut into rounds and the sliced onions. Sauté them in the butter and oil until the onions are browned, then pour off any excess fat and return the pieces of hare. Sprinkle with any remaining sea-soned flour, pour in the red wine and let it bubble gently for 10 minutes to reduce a little and drive off some of its alcohol.

A HANGING BRACE OF PHEASANT AND A GROUSE IN THE BAG AWAITING CLEANING AT THE END OF A DAY'S SHOOTING.

Meanwhile, preheat the oven to 150–170°C (300–325°F, Gas 2–3).

Add the spices and a good seasoning of pepper and salt, and pour in enough stock to bring the level two-thirds of the way up the meat. Let it come to the boil, then cover the casserole and cook for 1½ hours for a young hare or for 2 hours for a larger, older hare.

Remove the pieces of hare, carrots and onions with a slotted spoon and put them in a heated, deep serving dish. In a small pan, melt the butter and stir in the flour. Gradually add the hare gravy, stirring well between each addition; stir in the redcurrant jelly and when you have a smooth sauce remove the pan from the heat and taste for seasoning. Now stir in the blood of the hare and blend it in thoroughly. (If you find this very distaste-ful you can leave it out, but it does add to the richness of colour and flavour for which this traditional dish is so well known.)

Pour this gravy over the pieces of hare in the serving dish and keep hot for 5 minutes before serving to allow the dish to mellow.

Serve accompanied by plain boiled potatoes, watercress, perhaps a vegetable such as red cabbage, and redcurrant jelly. This dish reheats well, but do not boil or the sauce may separate.

HIGHLAND VENISON STEW

Venison is becoming more widely avail-able in supermarkets as well as in country markets, and is a good, low-fat meat. Scottish ghillies like to stew their venison to counteract the dryness of the meat.

1 kg (2 lb) venison from the leg or haunch
30 g (1 oz) seasoned flour
60 g (2 oz) bacon fat or 2 tablespoons vegetable oil
2 onions, coarsely chopped
2 rashers bacon, rinds removed, if necessary, and chopped
squeeze lemon juice
1 glass port
300 ml (½ pint) beef stock, preferably home-made (see page 20)
4 juniper berries, crushed
salt and freshly ground black pepper

*C*ut the trimmed venison into cubes and roll them in seasoned flour.

Melt the bacon fat or oil in a heavy casserole and fry the chopped onions and bacon until the onions are turning colour. Now add the meat and fry, turning the pieces of meat over in the fat as they brown. Add a squeeze of lemon juice, the port, stock, and juniper berries and any remaining flour.

Season with salt and pepper, cover and simmer for 1½ hours or until the venison is tender. Serve with baked potatoes and redcurrant or rowan jelly.

MEAT

*P*robably one of the most appetizing and enjoyable smells that can waft across the family table is the wonderful aroma of roast beef, done to a crisp on the outside and pink and juicy within. It also provides some kind of shared feeling of happiness amongst those who sit together to enjoy it. The only thing that may go wrong is often due to carver's nerves, particularly with joints that have a bone. To make carving easy it is vital to have a very sharp carving knife, with a blade not more than five or six inches long. A longer knife with a flexible blade is useful for ham, but not for carving a joint unless you want to cut very, very thin slices.

When choosing meat look for fine grain and, in beef, a rich deep colour. Conversely, the paler a leg or shoulder of lamb, the younger and therefore the more delicious it is likely to be. Pork or veal should also be pale, almost pearly in colour, with a bit of sparkle.

ROAST BEEF WITH YORKSHIRE PUDDING (PAGE 86) AND BRAISED LEEKS WITH CREAM (PAGE 120)

ROASTING MEAT

ALTHOUGH IT IS USUAL TO GIVE A TABLE FOR ROASTING MEAT, THIS DOESN'T ALWAYS WORK EXACTLY RIGHT. FIRST OF ALL, EVERYONE'S OVEN IS DIFFERENT; AN AGA COOKS DIFFERENTLY FROM A CONVENTIONAL OVEN AT THE SAME TEMPERATURE, AND FAN-ASSISTED OVENS COOK DIFFERENTLY AGAIN. THEN EACH PIECE OF MEAT YOU BUY IS AN INDIVIDUAL AND UNIQUE PIECE, DIFFERING IN SHAPE, SIZE, THICKNESS OF FAT, WEIGHT OF BONE, AGE AND MOISTURE CONTENT FROM THE ONE YOU BOUGHT LAST WEEK. A THICK PIECE OF MEAT WILL TAKE LONGER TO ROAST THAN A THIN ONE, BUT A ROLLED, BONED LOIN OF PORK IS QUITE DENSE, AND SO WILL TAKE AS LONG OR LONGER THAN A MUCH CHUNKIER LOOKING LOIN ON THE BONE. AFTER A WHILE YOU WILL START ADJUSTING BY 5 OR 10 MINUTES ACCORDING TO THE LOOK OF A JOINT; A LONG, SLENDER-LOOKING LEG OF LAMB WILL NEED A GOOD 20 MINUTES LESS THAN A SHORT, PLUMP ONE.

EVEN MORE IMPORTANT, PEOPLE LIKE THEIR MEAT COOKED IN DIFFERENT WAYS. SOME PEOPLE LIKE RARE BEEF AND WELL DONE LAMB. SOME LOVE EVERYTHING EXCEPT PORK TO HAVE A DECIDEDLY ROSE-PINK CENTRE, AND OTHERS LIKE PORK REALLY OVERCOOKED. SOME PEOPLE LIKE LONG SLOW ROASTING AND OTHERS, ESPECIALLY CHEFS, LIKE TO DO EVERYTHING AT THE HIGHEST TEMPERATURE AND AS FAST AS POSSIBLE, AND THEN TO LET IT RELAX AND RECOVER AFTERWARDS. SO ANY TIMES GIVEN ARE FOR A GENERAL GUIDE, RATHER THAN HARD AND FAST RULES.

THE BEST WAY TO DO ROAST BEEF

The best way to achieve a really well-roasted sirloin or rib of roast beef is to buy the very best beef that has been reared and hung in the traditional manner. This makes a difference; beef that hasn't been hung properly is not rewarding as it hasn't had time to develop flavour, succulence and tenderness.

The art of roasting is not learned by reading a recipe, but by practice. Even now, after twenty years or more of roasting meat, I can still get some nasty surprises.

Roughly speaking, a rare 3 kg (6 lb) rib or sirloin of beef on the bone will take 1½ hours to cook (15 minutes per 500 g/1 lb) at 190°C (375°F, Gas 5), and will need 30 minutes' rest at the end before carving, to give it time to relax. Rest the joint in a warm place, and keep it covered.

Smear the meat with butter and oil and sprinkle it with salt before you put it in the oven – some people like to put it on a small rack in the roasting tin. Baste and turn it every 20 minutes or so while it cooks. Keep an eye on it to see it is progressing well – if not, you can turn the oven up or down a little but this can depend on what else is in the oven with the beef. It doesn't roast as quickly in a very steamy oven, or if there are lots of potatoes around it, and other things taking up the heat.

Allow 3 kg (6 lb) beef on the bone for 10 people. Allow 2.2–2.5 kg (4½–5 lb) boned and rolled beef for 10 people.

Carving is much easier if the joint has been boned and rolled. If not, a prime sirloin of beef will have 2 sides to it, the top or sirloin and the undercut or fillet. Each person should get some of each.

Inexperienced carvers should remove the meat from the bone before attempting to slice it up. The ends will be for people who like it better done.

YORKSHIRE PUDDING

At one time Yorkshire pudding, the traditional English accompaniment to roast beef, was always served before the beef to fill the family and take the edge off their appetites, so that a small joint of beef would go round large numbers of children, grannies and aunts. Nowadays, we serve it with the beef, together with roast potatoes, a vegetable and a simple gravy made from the dripping.

If possible, make the batter 1 hour before you start to cook the pudding. Using an extra egg gives the pudding a very good rise, but perhaps a slightly less succulent texture.

SERVES 6

125 g (4 oz) plain flour
300 ml (½ pint) mixed milk and water
1 or 2 eggs, beaten
good pinch salt
3 tablespoons beef or pork dripping

*P*ut the flour in a bowl, gradually add the milk and water and the beaten egg or eggs, stirring constantly with a wooden spoon until the batter is smooth. Add a pinch of salt, beat well and allow the batter to stand for 1 hour.

Heat the dripping in a Yorkshire pudding tin or a small roasting tin in a hot oven, 220°C (425°F, Gas 7), beat the batter once more, pour into the hot fat and bake at the top of the oven over the meat for 30 minutes, until the pudding is well risen and brown.

GRILLED SIRLOIN STEAKS WITH HORSERADISH

One of our great traditional foods was meat; well-hung steak and chops grilled over or in front of a lovely bright fire – often a bed of coals – and served red hot with a good grill sauce. These sauces tended to be hot, too, containing mustard, Worcestershire sauce, cayenne and horseradish, or perhaps sharp pickles, capers and cucumbers. This kind of food was particularly enjoyed earlier in the century by businessmen, in the cosy steamy atmosphere of the many thriving chop-houses, grill rooms and inns, that provided them with an alternative to domesticity.

The horseradish sauce is much better if made with freshly grated horseradish root, although your eyes will stream whilst you grate it. You can sometimes buy fresh horseradish or find the roots growing – they thrive in allotments, on railway embankments and in old vegetable gardens. Otherwise you can buy it ready grated in jars.

250 g (8 oz) sirloin or rump steak per person (fillet steak is not tasty enough for this)
softened butter or oil
salt and freshly ground black pepper
fried potatoes and a salad, to serve

HORSERADISH SAUCE
2 tablespoons grated horseradish, fresh or preserved
1 tablespoon white wine vinegar
a little English mustard
pinch salt
pinch sugar
4 tablespoons double cream
cayenne pepper, to taste

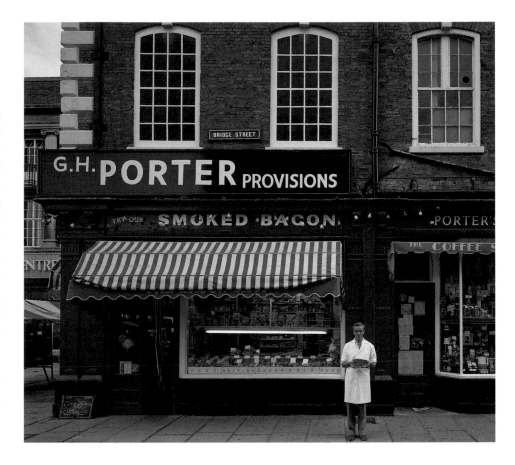

TO MAKE THE HORSERADISH SAUCE
Mix all the ingredients together in a bowl and taste a little to see if the balance of flavours is right. Keep at room temperature and use the same day.

GRILLING THE STEAK
Preheat the grill so it is really glowing before you start to cook.

Rub the steak all over with softened butter or vegetable oil. Put it close to the grill at first and allow it to become very frizzled on the outside, then move it a little further from the heat, sprinkle with salt and pepper and cook a few more minutes, turning it once. You can tell how well it is done by pressing it with your finger. A 'blue' steak will feel soft and yielding, 'rare' will be yielding but not too soft and wobbly, while a resilient or bouncy texture means the steak is well

A NOTTINGHAMSHIRE GROCER DISPLAYING HIS MEAT.

done right through.

Serve a beautifully grilled steak straight from the grill on a hot plate with the horseradish sauce, fried potatoes and a salad.

COOKING BEEF

USING THE CORRECT COOKING METHOD FOR A SPECIFIC CUT OF MEAT IS ONE WAY TO GUARANTEE DELICIOUS MEALS. IT IS NO GOOD TO PAN-FRY A FATTY PIECE OF BRISKET, FOR EXAMPLE, WHICH SHOULD BE GENTLY CASSEROLED OR POT ROASTED TO PRODUCE A TENDER RESULT.

BRISKET NEEDS LONG COOKING; BOIL, BRAISE, CASSEROLE, POT ROAST.

CHUCK NEEDS LONG COOKING; BRAISE, CASSEROLE, POT ROAST.

FILLET FRY, GRILL, ROAST

PRIME RIB ROAST

SILVERSIDE NEEDS LONG COOKING; CASSEROLE, POT ROAST.

SKIRT NEEDS LONG COOKING; CASSEROLE, POT ROAST.

STEAKS (FILLET, PORTERHOUSE, RUMP, SIRLOIN, T-BONE) FRY, GRILL, ROAST

TOPSIDE NOT EXPENSIVE AND CAN BE EATEN ROASTED IF KEPT VERY RARE, OTHERWISE IT NEEDS LONG COOKING; BRAISE, CASSEROLE, POT ROAST, ROAST.

SPICED BEEF

The British have always liked their spiced beef, and before Christmas the most enormous pieces of meat, weighing 10 kg (20 lb) or more, would be eaten as part of the 'cold collation' to which guests were treated any time of the day or night over the days of celebration. Although not often seen today, spiced beef is not a complicated dish to make. All that is needed is a week's advance notice.

SERVES 6

1 teaspoon ground cloves
1 teaspoon ground mace
1 teaspoon coarsely ground black pepper
1 teaspoon coarsely crushed allspice
1 dessertspoon dried thyme
250 g (8 oz) moist dark brown sugar
1 piece beef, such as silverside, top rump, thin flank or top rib, weighing 2.5–3 kg (5–6 lb)

250 g (8 oz) sea salt
15 g ($\frac{1}{2}$ oz) saltpetre
6 bay leaves
12 juniper berries, crushed
1 bunch fresh herbs – parsley and thyme
2 carrots, chopped
2 sticks celery, chopped
1 onion, chopped
2 wine glasses port
600 ml (1 pint) beef stock, preferably home-made (see page 20)
15 g ($\frac{1}{2}$ oz) powdered gelatine
1 large bunch fresh parsley, finely chopped

*M*ix the ground and crushed spices with the thyme. Mix half the mixture with the sugar. Cover the meat with it in a shallow earthenware dish, and leave to stand for 24 hours. Now add the salt, saltpetre, bay leaves and crushed juniper berries, rubbing them into the meat, and let it steep in the mixture for a week, rubbing and turning it daily.

When ready to cook the meat, rinse it and soak for 2–3 hours in cold water. Dry it well, spread the reserved ground and crushed spices over the inside of the beef, roll it up tightly and tie with string.

Put it into a heavy iron casserole which just fits it. Surround it with the bunch of herbs and the chopped carrots, celery and onion. Pour on the 2 glasses of port and the stock and cover tightly with its lid.

Cook for 4–5 hours very, very slowly with the liquid quietly simmering, turning the meat occasionally, or braise it in a very low oven, 150°C (300°F, Gas 2), for 4–5 hours, until very tender. Eat hot or, if wanted cold, allow to cool to lukewarm in the cooking liquid, then take it out and put it between 2 boards with a 500 g (1 lb) weight on top. Leave it overnight. The next day eat it plain or coat it with a beef jelly.

TO MAKE THE BEEF JELLY

Remove the fat from the top of the cooled cooking liquid. Strain, skim and taste the liquid. If it tastes too strong and salty dilute it with red wine or weak stock.

Measure 600 ml (1 pint) of the liquid. Heat 3–4 tablespoons. Put the gelatine in a cup with the heated liquid and place it in a shallow pan of hot water, over a moderate heat, stirring until it has completely dissolved. Add the dissolved gelatine and the chopped parsley to the measured amount of cooking liquid, and put it in the refrigerator, stirring it occasionally until it becomes thick and syrupy. Put the beef to chill at the same time.

As soon as the gelatine becomes thick, syrupy and almost set, remove the string from the beef and spoon the glaze over it. Chill and repeat this, giving 2 more coats so the beef has a nice thick glaze with green parsley embedded in it.

Pour the rest of the jelly into a shallow dish, allow to set in the fridge (if you are in a hurry, cool it quickly in the ice compartment). Then when the beef is to be served, cut the jelly into dice and pile round the beef on its serving dish.

Serve sliced, with pickles, such as pickled walnuts, and plenty of mustard. Hot jacket potatoes and green salad can be served with it.

BEEF WELLINGTON

SERVES 6–8

1 kg (2 lb) fillet of beef
250 g (8 oz) mushrooms
1 small onion
30 g (1 oz) butter
salt and freshly ground black pepper
1 dessertspoon finely chopped fresh parsley
500 g (1 lb) puff pastry
1 egg, beaten

Have the beef at room temperature. Chop the mushrooms and onion and soften them in the melted butter over a gentle heat. When the onion is tender, add the seasoning and chopped parsley and allow to cool in a bowl. Stir in half the beaten egg, and chill the mixture.

Preheat the oven to 220°C (425°F, Gas 7). Coat the beef lightly with oil and place it on a rack in a roasting tin. Sear it for 10 minutes in the oven (15 minutes if your piece of fillet is rather chunky and thick). Leave it to cool completely.

Cut the pastry into 2 pieces – 1 of three-quarters and 1 of one-quarter of its total weight. Roll out the larger piece on a floured board making an elongated oval shape, large enough almost to enclose the meat. Place the beef in the centre and spread the mushroom and onion mixture over the top of the meat.

Roll out the remaining piece of pastry into a long strip, large enough to make a cover. Bring the lower piece of pastry up and over the top of the beef. Brush the strip with water and press it over the top. Use any pastry trimmings to make rows of leaves along the top, attaching them with egg. Brush the pastry with egg to glaze it, prick holes in the top, and place the beef in a roasting tin in the middle of the oven. Bake for 15 minutes, cover loosely with foil, lower the oven temperature to 190°C (375°F, Gas 5) and bake a further 15 minutes. Leave to set for 15 minutes in a warm place before slicing about 2.5 cm (1 inch) thick.

You should have beautiful pink-centred beef with a golden crust. Serve with Horseradish Sauce (see page 158) to which you have added 4 tablespoons of double cream.

STEAK AND KIDNEY PIE

SERVES 6

1.2 kg (2½ lb) chuck steak or other good
braising steak
300 g (10 oz) ox kidney
2 onions
2 tablespoons lard or vegetable oil
30 g (1 oz) plain flour
150 ml (¼ pint) red wine
600 ml (1 pint) beef stock, preferably
home-made (see page 20)
dash Worcestershire sauce
1 teaspoon mushroom ketchup
bunch fresh herbs – thyme, parsley and
bay leaf
salt and freshly ground black pepper
350 g (12 oz) Rough Puff Pastry, made
from 180 g (6 oz) each butter and flour
(see page 187)
1 egg yolk, beaten, for glazing

*P*reheat the oven to 170°C (325°F,
Gas 3).

*Cut the beef into 4 cm (1½ inch) pieces
– keep them chunky and rather large so
they do not lose their succulence. Trim off
all the fat and sinew. Core the kidney and
cut into walnut-sized pieces. Peel and
chop the onions.*

*Heat the lard or vegetable oil in a
flameproof casserole, and when it starts to
smoke, fry the beef and kidney a few
pieces at a time, so they are browned on
all sides. Remove the pieces to a dish as
they brown. When all the meat is done,
brown the onions in the same fat.*

*Return the meat to the casserole and
sprinkle on the flour. Let it brown, then
add the red wine and beef stock, stirring
to incorporate the flour and deglaze the
bottom of the casserole. Add the Worcestershire sauce, mushroom ketchup and the
herbs and seasonings and bring to a slow
simmer on the top of the stove. Then cover
the casserole and transfer to the oven to*

*simmer for 1½–2 hours – test to see if it is
done after 1½ hours. Remove from the
oven, take out the herbs and leave to cool.
Taste and adjust the seasoning if
necessary.*

*Transfer the meat to a 25 cm (10
inch) pie dish with a pie-funnel in the
centre. If you don't think there is enough
meat to hold up the crust, put a few
peeled and quartered par-boiled potatoes
on top of the meat and this will do the
trick beautifully (and the potatoes will
taste delicious). Preheat the oven to
220°C (425°F, Gas 7).*

*Roll out the pastry. Brush the edge of
the pie dish with egg glaze and cut some
strips of pastry to fit round the rim of the
dish. Brush the strips with glaze, put the
remaining pastry on top, trim the edge,
scallop it and knock it up with the blade
of a knife so that the actual cut edge looks
as deep as possible. Make a hole in the
centre and cut some leaves from the trimmings to decorate the top. Brush the pie
top with egg glaze, place the leaves on top
and brush again.*

*Cook in the oven for 12 minutes, then
lower the temperature to 180°C (350°F,
Gas 4) for 30 minutes. Cover lightly with
foil if it shows signs of over-browning.*

*Serve steak and kidney pie with a green
vegetable such as purple sprouting broccoli
or lightly cooked buttered green cabbage
and perhaps some small baked potatoes, or
with mashed potatoes. Watercress, Chicory
and Hazelnut Salad (see page 46) is also
a good accompaniment.*

VARIATION

*The steak and kidney pie can also have
mushrooms in it. Sauté them lightly
before you fry the onions, then keep them
on one side and put them into the pie dish
when you add the meat.*

STEAK AND KIDNEY PUDDING

SERVES 6

1 kg (2 lb) beef, including chuck steak
or other juicy stewing steak, and a
piece of skirt
250 g (8 oz) ox kidney
30 g (1 oz) seasoned flour
125 g (4 oz) button mushrooms,
cleaned and trimmed
1 tablespoon Worcestershire sauce
dash Tabasco sauce
1 tablespoon mushroom ketchup
(optional)
beef stock, preferably home-made (see
page 20)
salt and coarsely ground black pepper

FOR THE SUET CRUST

125 g (4 oz) shredded suet
250 g (8 oz) self-raising flour
salt

PASTRY

*Mix the suet, flour and salt in a bowl and
then add just enough cold water to bind it
– don't add too much at first: this mixture
should be light and spongy, not wet. Roll
it out, keeping back about one quarter for
the lid, and line a buttered 1.2 litre (2
pint) pudding basin.*

FILLING

*Trim the meat of fat and sinews and cut it
into cubes. Cut the kidney into pieces the
size of small walnuts. Roll the beef and
kidney in seasoned flour, mix with the
mushrooms and put into the basin. Mix
the Worcestershire sauce, Tabasco and
mushroom ketchup together and pour it
in, then add enough well-seasoned beef
stock or water to come two thirds to three
quarters of the way up the sides. Use
plenty of pepper in the seasoning. Moisten*

two thirds of the way up the basin, and must be topped up as it boils away. If the pudding leaks a bit, don't worry. Boil, covered, for 4–5 hours.

Lift the pudding out of the pan and remove the foil. Wrap the basin in a clean white napkin, with the top crust showing fluffy and slightly browned from its collar of white linen. If the crust has come in contact with water, it may be pale and glistening; it will still be delicious to eat.

Serve the fragrant pudding with a robust vegetable such as spring greens. A good claret is the best drink to serve with steak and kidney pudding.

BEEF AND CABBAGE

It is rather difficult to give exact quantities for a dish like this. However, if you have some rosy-pink roast beef left over, try serving it this way.

1 head green cabbage
salt and freshly ground black pepper
at least 250 g (8 oz) rare roast beef
15–30 g (½–1 oz) butter
1–2 tablespoons gravy from the beef
Worcestershire sauce

Cut away the outer leaves of the cabbage, quarter it and core. Drop the quarters into plenty of boiling salted water. Boil rapidly, uncovered, for 10 minutes, until the cabbage just turns translucent green. Drain well and chop roughly.

Slice the beef and cut into strips.

Heat the butter in a frying pan, add the cabbage and stir it round until it is hot and buttery all the way through. Add the beef, stir briefly, then add the gravy and 1–2 dashes of Worcestershire sauce. Stir round once or twice rapidly over a high heat until the ingredients are all piping hot, season.

the top edge of the crust.

Roll out the remaining pastry to make a lid. Cover the pudding, press firmly to seal, then trim and roll the edges over inwards, pressing lightly.

To steam the pudding, pleat a piece of foil and cover the top of the pudding loosely with it, tying it round under the

A FARMER WITH HIS GIANT CABBAGES.

rim of the basin with string. Make a handle by passing the string across the top 2 or 3 times – not too tightly as the pudding must have room to expand. Lower into a large pan of boiling water with a close-fitting lid; the water should come

BROWN BRAISED BEEF WITH DUMPLINGS

The interesting thing about this adaptation of an old recipe called Brown Braise (which called for trimmings of meat rather than a piece of meat itself, and must have been rather like the stew that was offered in British restaurants during the war, where the customers' meat coupons bought them a plate of delicious gravy) is the combination of herbs used. Thyme is predictable, sweet marjoram less so and basil rather a surprise, as it is difficult to grow in the British climate. However, it is an old favourite in Britain and was once an important ingredient in, of all things, mock turtle soup. The herbs are dried, giving a very different flavour to the fresh basil leaves strewn on tomato salad in the summer.

SERVES 4–6

1.2 kg (2½ lb) chuck steak
4 large carrots
2 onions and 3 shallots, or 3 onions
small stick celery
sprinkling plain flour
45 g (1½ oz) butter
½ teaspoon each dried thyme, sweet or knotted marjoram and basil
1 tablespoon chopped fresh parsley
4 anchovies in oil, well drained and chopped
sprinkling grated nutmeg or ground mace
salt and freshly ground black pepper
150 ml (¼ pint) dry white wine
600 ml (1 pint) beef stock, preferably home-made (see page 20), or water

BROWN BRAISED BEEF WITH DUMPLINGS (BACK); BRAISED OXTAIL WITH HARICOT BEANS (PAGE 104)

NORFOLK DUMPLINGS

1 egg
150 ml (¼ pint) milk
200–250 g (7–8 oz) self-raising flour
½ teaspoon salt
1 tablespoon chopped fresh parsley

Cut the trimmed beef into 2 cm (¾ inch) cubes. Cut the carrots into .5 cm (¼ inch) slices and roughly chop the onions and shallots and celery. Flour the meat generously.

Melt 30 g (1 oz) of the butter in a fairly small flameproof casserole (this would once have been called a stewpot). When it starts to brown add the steak, one quarter at a time, and fry the pieces, not too fast, removing them as they are browned and adding the herbs and anchovies towards the end. Use more butter if necessary.

When all the pieces are browned, return them to the casserole, add the vegetables and seasonings and stir everything over a low heat for a few minutes. Then add the wine and stock. Cover the casserole and cook for 1½–1¾ hours at a gentle simmer.

TO MAKE THE NORFOLK DUMPLINGS

Beat the egg with the milk, and gradually add to the flour to make a very thick batter. Beat well, adding salt and chopped parsley. Drop a few teaspoonfuls of the mixture at a time into boiling water and lift out when they float – after 4–5 minutes.

Serve the dumplings on the stew. Alternatively, you can put teaspoons of the mixture on top of the simmering stew, cover the pan and simmer until they swell and cook through – about 10 minutes.

ROAST LOIN OF PORK WITH CRACKLING

The best part of a pork loin is the piece with the kidney underneath.

SERVES 6

1.7–2 kg (3½–4lb) loin of pork, with the bone chined and skin scored
15 g (½ oz) butter
2 tablespoons vegetable oil

GRAVY

1 tablespoon plain flour
2 tablespoons sherry
3 tablespoons dry red wine
1 bay leaf
300 ml (½ pint) stock, preferably home-made (see page 20)
salt and freshly ground black pepper

AN OLD-FASHIONED BUTCHER'S SHOPFRONT
IN THE COTSWOLDS.

*I*t is best not to overcook pork; unfortunately, because it is common knowledge that it should not be eaten underdone, it is nearly always overdone. You want to cook it only until it has a white, pearly sheen (it is pink when underdone and pale beige when overdone). It should still be succulent and juicy, but the crackling should be very crisp.

Start by preheating the oven to 220°C (425°F, Gas 7). Rub the crackling with a little piece of butter – it gives a better result than oil. Don't sprinkle it with salt, as this will toughen the crackling. Put the remaining butter and oil in a roasting tin with the pork on top.

Roast the pork at the high temperature for 10–15 minutes, then lower the temperature to 190°C (375°F, Gas 5). From this point allow 20 minutes per 500 g (1 lb) and 20 minutes over for a small joint. Don't baste the crackling, just let it cook and it will be crisp and delicious.

When the joint is ready, transfer it to a serving platter, keep it hot and let it rest for about 15 minutes while you make the gravy. Spoon some of the fat off the roasting tin if necessary, then sprinkle in the flour and let it brown, stirring up all the sediment. Add the sherry, red wine and bay leaf, keep cooking it over a medium heat until reduced somewhat, then add the stock, half at a time, stirring and tasting. Add seasoning and serve with the pork. It should be delicious, especially if you use good rich stock.

Onion and sage sauce is the traditional accompaniment but I prefer to serve apple and sage sauce – just sprinkle a little chopped sage in with the Baked Apple Sauce on page 158.

ROAST LOIN OF PORK WITH CRACKLING

ROAST VEAL

SERVES 6

1.5 kg (3 lb) rolled and tied loin or
boned shoulder of veal
60 g (2 oz) butter
1 tablespoon plain flour
250 g (8 oz) streaky bacon rashers,
rinds removed if necessary
24 button onions
3–4 tablespoons dry white wine
300 ml (½ pint) veal or chicken stock,
preferably home-made (see page 20)
salt and freshly ground black pepper
lemon juice (optional)

*P*reheat the oven to 170°C (325°F,
Gas 3).

Spread the veal with butter and
sprinkle it with flour. Place it in a roasting tin and cover the top with rashers of
bacon. Put it in the middle of the oven
and roast, basting frequently for 30
minutes per 500 g (1 lb). After 1 hour,
cover the top loosely with a sheet of foil.

Peel the onions and drop them into
boiling salted water for 5 minutes. Drain
them and put them round the meat for
the last 30 minutes of roasting. When the
meat is done put it on a heated platter
with the well-drained onions round the
sides. Keep it hot and leave for 20 minutes to settle and make it easier to carve.

Meanwhile, skim the fat from the
juices in the roasting tin, add the white
wine and let it boil down, stirring and
scraping the bottom of the tin. Now add
the stock and simmer for a few minutes,
season with salt and pepper, and if necessary a squeeze of lemon juice. Serve the
gravy very hot.

Serve with new potatoes or creamy
mashed potatoes, and peas or spinach.
Some white button mushrooms, lightly
cooked in butter are also a good accompaniment to this dish.

STEWED VEAL WITH GREEN PEAS

This has a delicious old-fashioned flavour, that has been rather forgotten
recently. Veal is a very good meat for
stewing as it has a gelatinous texture
which makes a good velvety gravy.

SERVES 4

1 kg (2 lb) pie veal
seasoned flour
15 g (½ oz) butter
1 tablespoon oil
1 small glass white wine
4 spring onions, cut into short lengths
bunch fresh herbs – bay, thyme and
parsley
generous pinches ground mace,
allspice, cloves, black pepper
grated rind of ½ lemon
salt and freshly ground black pepper
about 600 ml (1 pint) light chicken
stock, preferably home-made (see page
20), or water
350 g (12 oz) shelled green peas, fresh
or frozen
1 tablespoon plain flour
30 g (1 oz) butter, softened
2 teaspoons lemon juice

*C*ut the veal into large pieces, trimming them well. Roll the pieces in
seasoned flour and fry them in the butter
and oil in a casserole a few at a time.
Transfer them to a dish when they are
lightly browned all over.

Pour the wine into the casserole and
scrape up all the sediment. Let it boil for
1–2 minutes, then lower the heat and
throw in the spring onions. Return the
veal to the pan and add the herbs, spices
and grated lemon rind. Season, add stock
or water barely to cover the meat, cover
the pan and simmer for 1–1½ hours, until
the veal is meltingly tender.

Meanwhile, cook the peas briefly in boiling salted water. Work the flour into the butter to make a smooth paste.

When the veal is ready, stir the peas into the gravy and then add half the flour and butter in little pieces, stirring it well over a low heat for several minutes. See if the sauce is as you like it; if it is still too thin, add a little more of the flour and butter paste. Lastly, stir in the lemon juice and taste for seasoning. Serve very hot with boiled new potatoes or mashed potatoes.

ROAST LEG OF LAMB

This method of cooking allows 15 minutes per 500 g (1 lb) and gives a very succulent, deep rose-pink finish to the lamb when it is carved. For well-done lamb allow 20 minutes per 500 g (1 lb). The resting time allows the meat to relax, making it easier to carve, and gives a more even colour to the slices.

SERVES AT LEAST 8

1 leg of lamb weighing about 3 kg (6 lb), including the knuckle bone
60 g (2 oz) butter, softened
90 g (3 oz) fresh white breadcrumbs
3 tablespoons chopped fresh parsley
2 teaspoons dried marjoram
1 teaspoon dried thyme
$\frac{1}{2}$ teaspoon salt

GRAVY

3 tablespoons red wine
300 ml ($\frac{1}{2}$ pint) chicken or other stock, preferably home-made (see page 20)

Preheat the oven to 220°C (425°F, Gas 7).

Spread the lamb all over with butter. Mix together the breadcrumbs, herbs and salt and press them into the butter all over

A FIELD OF WELSH LAMB.

the leg of lamb. (In the past the bread-crumbs and melted butter flavoured with herbs were strewn over the meat as it turned on a spit in front of the fire; this protected the meat from scorching and helped to keep it juicy. This coating forms the same function in the oven.)

Cook on a rack over a roasting tin in the oven for 15 minutes, then lower the heat to 180°C (350°F, Gas 4) and cook for a further 1–1¼ hours. Allow the lamb to rest in a warm place for 30 minutes before carving.

TO MAKE THE GRAVY

While the lamb is resting, take the roasting tin which has caught all the juices and falling crumbs. Spoon off most of the fat and add the red wine. Bring the liquid

to the boil, let it reduce by half and then add the chicken stock or other good, well-flavoured stock. Reduce again, stirring the bottom of the tin to release all the syrupy, caramelized juices that have collected there. When reduced to about half, strain the gravy into a heated gravy boat and serve very, very hot with the lamb sliced fairly thickly if very pink, and thinly if well done. Serve with scalloped potatoes and roast winter vegetables (see page 118) in winter, and new potatoes and peas, or,

GUARD OF HONOUR

This is a beautiful and traditional dish, made from best ends of lamb, with the bones trimmed and crossed in the air like swords at a military wedding. It is not a complicated dish and looks pretty and festive.

SERVES 4

2 best ends of lamb with 8 cutlets each
1 onion, sliced
1 tablespoon vegetable oil
60 g (2 oz) butter
1 glass sherry

STUFFING

1 onion
30 g (1 oz) butter
180 g (6 oz) button mushrooms
grated rind of ½ lemon
salt and freshly ground black pepper
cayenne pepper
60 g (2 oz) white bread, crusts removed
milk
1 teaspoon chopped marjoram, thyme and chives
2 tablespoons finely chopped fresh parsley

GRAVY

1 dessertspoon plain flour
300 ml (½ pint) good stock, preferably home-made (see page 20)
pinch sugar
salt and freshly ground black pepper
vinegar (optional)

TO PREPARE GUARD OF HONOUR

IF NOT ALREADY DONE, HAVE THE BUTCHER CHINE THE BEST ENDS, COMPLETELY REMOVING THE BACKBONE (RESERVE THE BONE FOR THE ROASTING TIN). SKIN THE MEAT. TRIM THE FAT FROM THE TOP 4 CM (1½ INCH) OF THE CUTLET BONES VERY CAREFULLY WITH A SHARP KNIFE SO THEY ARE NEAT AND BARE; BE SURE TO TRIM AWAY ALL FAT AND MEAT FROM BETWEEN THE BONES. SCORE THE OUTSIDE OF THE FAT DIAGONALLY IN BOTH DIRECTIONS TO MAKE DIAMOND SHAPES: THIS ENABLES THE FAT TO COOK QUICKLY AND BECOME CRISP. PLACE THE TWO BEST ENDS STANDING UP IN THE ROASTING TIN WITH TIPS INTERLACED.

*P*repare the guard of honour (see left). Preheat the oven to 220°C (425°F, Gas 7). Now stand the best ends on top of the sliced onion and chine bones in a roasting tin with the bone ends upwards and crossed over at the tips. This forms the guard of honour.

Coat the joints with oil and then smear them with butter. Cover the tops of the bones with foil to prevent them from burning. Put into the middle of the oven and roast for 25 minutes, then baste the joint and pour the sherry into the roasting tin. Cook for a further 15 minutes, basting occasionally.

While the lamb is roasting, make the stuffing, which goes in after the meat is cooked. Chop the onion finely and soften it in the butter for about 10 minutes without browning. Now add the finely chopped mushrooms, grated lemon rind and seasoning of salt, pepper and cayenne. Cook for 5 minutes more. Cut the bread into cubes, soak in a little milk, squeeze dry and crumble.

Add the mushroom mixture, the herbs and parsley and mix to a crumbly soft stuffing. Keep hot.

When the guard of honour is cooked, remove the protective foil, press the stuffing into the central cavity and place the meat in position on a heated serving dish. Keep hot in the oven, turned right down and with the door slightly open.

To make the gravy, remove the chine bones from the pan, skim off the fat from the juices and stir in the flour; let it cook for a minute, scraping up the caramelized juices in the bottom of the tin. Add the stock, a small pinch of sugar, and seasoning, and simmer until the gravy is the consistency of thin cream. Serve separately. If necessary, a tiny drop of vinegar can be added to sharpen the flavour.

Carve the lamb downwards between the bones, serving 4 cutlets to each person. Put them on each plate, crossed over at the bone end, with a tablespoonful of the stuffing in between. Lightly cooked French beans or spinach tossed in butter make a good accompaniment to this dish. Serve with mint sauce or redcurrant jelly (in the past this was reserved for mutton, but it is also excellent with lamb).

LAMB CURRY

SERVES 4–6

1 kg (2 lb) cubed lean lamb (this is the quantity you will get from 1 shoulder)

3 onions

3 cloves garlic

2–3 tablespoons oil or softened butter

2 tablespoons hot Madras curry powder

2 teaspoons curry paste

2 teaspoons ground coriander

1 teaspoon ground cumin

½ teaspoon, or less, ground chilli

2.5 cm (1 inch) cube fresh root ginger, finely chopped

600 ml (1 pint) lamb stock, preferably from the bones and trimmings of the shoulder, well skimmed

1½ teaspoons salt

2 tablespoons coconut milk (optional)

*T*rim the meat well and peel and chop the onions and garlic. Heat the oil or butter in a flameproof casserole and fry the onions and garlic until pale golden. Add the curry powder and paste and spices and fry for 1–2 minutes, then add the ginger and the meat. Fry over a moderate heat so the meat is browned and sealed on all sides. Add the lamb stock and salt, and a little coconut milk, if using this.

Bring to a simmer and cook gently on top of the stove or in the oven at 170°C (325°F, Gas 3) for 1½ hours or until tender. Stir frequently and allow the liquid to cook down until it is rich and thick – just enough to bathe the meat; this curry is a dryish one rather than a wet one.

Serve with hot lemon pickle or hot lime pickle and mango chutney, and with rice. Other good side dishes to serve with this curry are quartered lemons, some shredded lettuce with quartered tomatoes and grilled or fried poppadums.

LAMB CURRY

IRISH STEW

SERVES 4

750 g–1 kg (1½–2 lb) best end and
middle neck of English lamb, cut into
chops and well trimmed
500 g (1 lb) potatoes
250 g (8 oz) onions
salt and freshly ground black pepper
chopped fresh thyme, to taste
450 ml (¾ pint) stock, preferably home-
made (see page 20)
chopped fresh parsley

Preheat the oven to 170°C (325°F, Gas 3).

Cut all the larger pieces of fat away from the chops. Peel the potatoes, cutting them into fairly large pieces, and peel and chop the onions rather coarsely.

Put a layer of chops in a 2.4 litre (4 pint) casserole, season them well with salt, pepper and thyme. Then put in a layer of onions and a layer of potatoes. Repeat these layers, add stock, cover the casserole with a piece of buttered foil and the lid, and cook for at least 2 hours or until the meat is really tender.

Serve the stew sprinkled with liberal quantities of chopped fresh parsley.

SHEPHERD'S PIE

Shepherd's pie is always made with left-over roast lamb and can be delicious, juicy and full of flavour, or dry and boring according to how much trouble you take. Cottage pie is the same sort of thing but made with beef – either fresh minced beef or cold roast beef. You can use this recipe with either.

SERVES 6

750 g (1½ lb) roast lamb, preferably
medium-rare
2 onions
1 tablespoon vegetable oil
30 g (1 oz) butter
30 g (1 oz) plain flour
4 tablespoons dry red wine
250 ml (8 fl oz) gravy or stock,
preferably home-made (see page 20)
½ teaspoon dried thyme
½ teaspoon well-pounded dried
rosemary
Tabasco sauce and/or Worcestershire
sauce
1 teaspoon tomato purée
salt and freshly ground black pepper

MASHED POTATOES
750 g (1½ lb) potatoes
60 g (2 oz) butter
generous 150 ml (¼ pint) milk, hot
salt and freshly ground black pepper

TO MAKE THE MASHED POTATOES
Boil the potatoes in well-salted water until very tender, drain well and mash, adding plenty of butter and hot milk. Give them a good beating to make them really smooth and creamy and season well.

TO MAKE THE FILLING
Preheat the oven to 180°C (350°F, Gas 4). Mince or chop the lamb not too finely (coarser pieces do not dry out so quickly). Peel and chop the onions. Heat the oil and butter in a large frying pan and fry the onions until golden brown. Add the lamb and let it brown in places, then sprinkle on the flour and brown that too as much as is possible – most of it disappears into the meat in some mysterious way.

Now add the liquids, first the red wine which should bubble and sizzle, then the stock. Stir it in well, deglazing the pan, and add the herbs and seasonings, including Tabasco and/or Worcestershire sauce to taste and the tomato purée. Simmer for about 10 minutes, add more stock if necessary, then transfer to a 23 cm (9 inch) pie dish.

Cover lightly with mashed potatoes – do not smooth it down. Dot the top with little bits of butter and cook for 30 minutes, until browned and crusty on top.

TOAD-IN-THE-HOLE

Traditionally, the friendly sounding 'toad' was another good, filling recipe for using up leftover meat, but now it is always made with bangers. For the best results, use really good-quality sausages with plenty of character to make this filling dish.

SERVES 4

15 g (½ oz) lard or oil
500 g (1 lb) sausages

FOR THE BATTER
180 g (6 oz) plain flour
pinch salt
2 eggs
600 ml (1 pint) milk and water mixed

*M*ake the batter 1 hour before you start to cook the dish. Put the flour into a bowl with the salt, make a well in the centre and break in the eggs. Beat them into the flour, gradually beating in the milk and water to make a smooth, creamy batter. Leave it to stand for 1 hour.

Preheat the oven to 220°C (425°F, Gas 7). Melt the lard or oil in a hot frying pan and brown the sausages all over – they look and taste better if they are pan-fried, rather than browned in

TOAD-IN-THE-HOLE

the oven.

Pour the fat and sausages into a 30 cm (12 inch) roasting tin and put in the oven to heat through. Pour in the batter and return it to the oven, then when the batter is nicely puffed and golden brown, lower the temperature to 190°C (375°, Gas 5) and cook for 35–40 minutes altogether. Cut into individual portions to serve at once.

TRADITIONAL SAUSAGES

YOU CAN ELEVATE A HUMBLE TOAD-IN-THE-HOLE, LEFT, OR BANGERS AND MASH TO DINNER PARTY FARE BY BUYING TOP-QUALITY SAUSAGES. TRY THESE TRADITIONAL BANGERS:
CAMBRIDGE MINCED PORK WITH HERBS AND SPICES.
CUMBERLAND CONTINUOUS LINK OF CHOPPED PORK WITH HERBS AND SPICES.
OXFORD MINCED BEEF, PORK AND VEAL WITH HERBS AND SPICES.
LINCOLNSHIRE SAGE-FLAVOURED MINCED PORK AND CEREAL WITH SPICES.

BRAISED OXTAIL WITH HARICOT BEANS

I like oxtail to be overcooked, so that it falls off the bone in succulent pieces. If it isn't quite done, the bones bounce around the plate while you struggle to detach the meat, and it can all be very awkward. The gravy should be gelatinous and very velvety.

If you prefer to soak your beans overnight rather than use the quicker method of preparation in the recipe, allow three days to make this dish.

SERVES 6

2 oxtails, jointed
250 g (8 oz) dried haricot beans
3–4 carrots
2 sticks celery
2 onions
1 tablespoon plain flour
60 g (2 oz) butter and a little oil
good seasoning of marjoram, thyme and celery salt
2–3 bay leaves
salt
freshly ground black pepper
beef stock, preferably home-made (see page 20)
150 ml (¼ pint) dry red wine or port

THE DAY BEFORE

Soak the oxtails for 2–3 hours. Meanwhile, if you have not soaked them overnight, put the beans in a pan, well covered with water. Bring them to the boil, then lower the heat and simmer for 5 minutes. Remove from the heat, cover the pan and leave it to cool. By the time the beans have cooled down they should be ready to cook, unless they are very old.

Slice the carrots, celery and peeled onions. Drain and dry the oxtails and dust them with flour.

Heat the butter and oil in a large casserole and fry the pieces of oxtail a few at a time, until they have a nice dark crust. Remove the oxtails, add the sliced vegetables and let them soften for a few minutes. Put back the oxtails, cover with stock, add the drained beans, herbs and seasoning and simmer very slowly, with a tilted lid, for 3 hours. Add a little beef stock if the gravy evaporates too rapidly. Cool and leave overnight in the refrigerator.

THE DAY OF SERVING

Remove the fat from the top. Add the wine or port and simmer for 1 or 2 hours before serving with puréed celeriac. You can add fresh vegetables for the second half of the cooking if you like.

CALVES' LIVER AND BACON

Lambs' liver can also be cooked in exactly this way; it is best in spring with the new season's lamb.

allow 125 g (4 oz) calves' liver per person, sliced .5 cm (¼ inch) thick
2 rashers smoked back bacon per person
2 teaspoons olive oil
2 teaspoons butter
plain flour for dusting
salt and freshly ground black pepper

*T*rim the liver, removing the thin membrane from the edges of each slice and any large pipes. Cut the rinds off the bacon and nick the fat with scissors.

Heat the oil and butter in a good, well-seasoned frying pan that doesn't stick. Allow the bacon to cook for about 2 minutes on each side, then transfer it to a heated serving dish and keep it hot.

Dust the slices of liver lightly with flour and shake off any excess. Put them straight into the hot bacon fat and oil, and brown fairly gently for 3–4 minutes on each side. (Thicker slices will need a little longer.) As you turn the pieces, season the cooked side with salt and pepper.

Serve with the bacon, fried potatoes and perhaps watercress or a fried tomato.

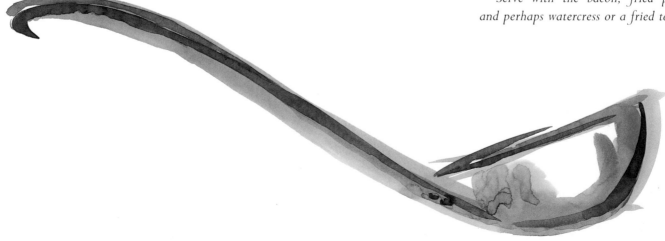

GRILLED KIDNEYS WITH PARSLEY BUTTER

SERVES 4

8–12 lambs' or 4 pigs' kidneys
salt and freshly ground black pepper
cayenne pepper
30 g (1 oz) butter, melted
1 bunch watercress, to garnish

PARSLEY BUTTER
60 g (2 oz) butter
2 tablespoons finely chopped fresh parsley
juice of ½ lemon
salt and freshly ground black pepper

*T*o make the parsley butter, leave the butter to soften to room temperature in a bowl. Chop the parsley finely. Mash the butter with a fork, add the parsley, lemon juice and salt and pepper and mix until smooth. Leave to set in a cold place. Preheat the grill.

Rinse and pick over the watercress, and shake it dry in a cloth. Now skin the kidneys if they have not already been skinned. Split them down the rounded side, and trim the central core but do not quite divide them. Run a skewer through the back of each so that the kidneys stay flat during cooking. Season them highly with salt, pepper and cayenne, then brush with melted butter.

Grill the kidneys for 4–5 minutes on each side, brushing with more butter if they seem dry.

Serve sizzling hot with a walnut of the parsley butter melting on top of each kidney, and a small neat bunch of watercress on each plate to dip into the juices.

GAMMON STEAKS WITH DRY CIDER SAUCE

SERVES 4

4 thick gammon steaks, weighing
180–250 g (6–8 oz) each, rinds removed
2 teaspoons Dijon mustard
2 teaspoons brown sugar
300 ml (½ pint) dry cider
1 teaspoon cornflour
2 tablespoons double cream
salt
freshly ground black pepper
fresh parsley, to garnish

*S*oak the gammon steaks in water for 1 hour. Remove them and pat them dry with kitchen paper. Make a paste with the mustard, sugar and a little cider, and spread the gammon steaks with the mixture, leaving them to soak up the flavour for 20 minutes.

Meanwhile, preheat the oven to 200°C (400°F, Gas 6).

Put the steaks, coated with the mustard mixture, in the bottom of a casserole and pour on the cider. Bake for 20 minutes.

When the gammon steaks are cooked through, strain off the liquid into a small saucepan.

Stir in the cornflour dissolved in 2 tablespoons water and stir while you bring the mixture to the boil. Lower the heat and then simmer gently for 5 minutes. When the cornflour is cooked stir the double cream into the sauce. Taste for seasoning and add salt and pepper to taste.

Pour the sauce over the gammon steaks, garnish with parsley and serve hot.

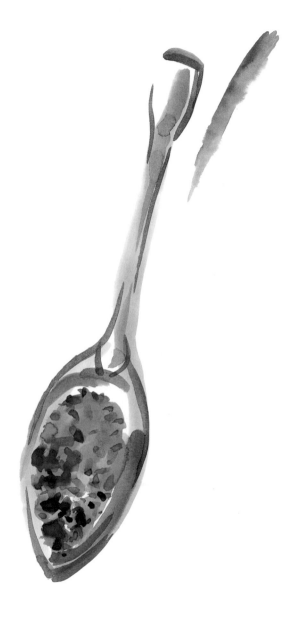

COOKING A GAMMON OR HAM

Many people are in a state of confusion about what is gammon and what is ham. Technically, gammon is a joint cut from the hind quarter of a side of bacon, while for ham the hind quarter is cut and cured separately from the rest of the pig. Speciality hams such as York, Bradenham or Suffolk are still cut and cured separately by traditional methods. You will find, however, that it is perfectly correct nowadays to call the cured hind leg of the bacon pig gammon when it is served hot, but ham when cold.

A small piece of gammon or uncooked ham takes more time to cook per 500 g (1 lb) than a large one. Anything under 2.5 kg (5 lb) takes 30 minutes per 500 g (1 lb) and 30 minutes over. We usually buy a piece weighing about 2.5 kg (5 lb) and I allow 30 minutes per 500 g (1 lb) without extra time.

Anything larger gets a relatively shorter time. These times come from a chart compiled by the Ministry of Agriculture and Fisheries, and reproduced from Jane Grigson's *Charcuterie and French Pork Cookery*.

2.5–5 kg (5–10 lb) 2½ hours
5 kg (10 lb) 3 hours
6 kg (12 lb) 3½ hours
7 kg (14 lb) 3¾ hours
8 kg (16 lb) 4 hours
9 kg (18 lb) 4¼ hours
10 kg (20 lb) 4½ hours
11 kg (22 lb) 4¾ hours
12 kg (24 lb) 5 hours

*W*eigh the joint before soaking to calculate the time you will have to allow. There is nothing more disappoint- *ing than very salty ham, so always soak the ham or gammon thoroughly unless the label specifically states you will not need to do so. Soak a small piece, under 2 kg (4 lb), overnight: a larger 2.5–5 kg (5–10 lb) piece for 24 hours, changing the water frequently. A whole ham will need 3 days' soaking and a Bradenham ham takes up to a week to soak properly. Change the water regularly and keep it in a cool place or the meat may go off.*

When the joint is ready to cook, put it into a large pan and cover with cold water. Bring to the boil, then lower the heat to a simmer and skim. Add a carrot, 2 leeks, a couple of onions and sticks of celery and a bunch of herbs. Count the cooking time from this point. Like all so called 'boiled' meat, ham should never be boiled, but gently simmered with a nice rhythmic, lazy 'blop' coming up at intervals as you watch. Taste the liquid occasionally and if it starts to taste unpalatably salty in spite of all your soaking, change it; replacing it with fresh boiling water.

Test the meat with a skewer when it is time for it to be done; it should feel quite firm but not rubbery. Remove the pan from the heat.

TO SERVE HOT

If you want to glaze the joint, remove the ham from its cooking liquid about 30 minutes before the end of the cooking time. Lift it out on to a dish and remove the skin, leaving the fat intact. Score the fat in a diamond pattern, stick cloves into the scores and coat with a mixture of 1 tablespoon Dijon mustard, 30 g (1 oz) soft dark brown sugar, the grated rind of 1 lemon or orange and a squeeze of lemon or orange juice beaten together. Pour a little oil and perhaps a few tablespoons of cider or apple juice or of the cooking liquid into a roasting tin, put the ham, fat side up, on top, and roast at 190°C (375°F, Gas 5) for 20–30 minutes or until glazed a rich, shiny, mahogany colour. Serve this with Cumberland Sauce (see page 156) or Parsley Sauce (see page 155).*

Alternatively, you can complete the cooking in the water, then simply remove the skin and serve the joint as it is.

TO SERVE COLD

Either glaze the ham as above, and let it get cold, or let it cool in the cooking liquid, then remove it. Take off the skin, dry the fat and press dried breadcrumbs into it all over – use home-made breadcrumbs, the bought ones are a horrible bright orange and make everything look the same.

For a whole ham, either buy a frill to put over the knuckle, which makes it easy to hold whilst you are carving, or make one out of white paper. If you are keeping a cooked ham for a period of time and continuing to cut from it, keep the cut surface covered to prevent it drying out.

Serve the ham with Cumberland Sauce (see page 156) or with home-made chutney, baked potatoes and salad – chicory and orange is a good combination.

GLAZED GAMMON AND BROAD BEANS WITH HAM (PAGE 111)

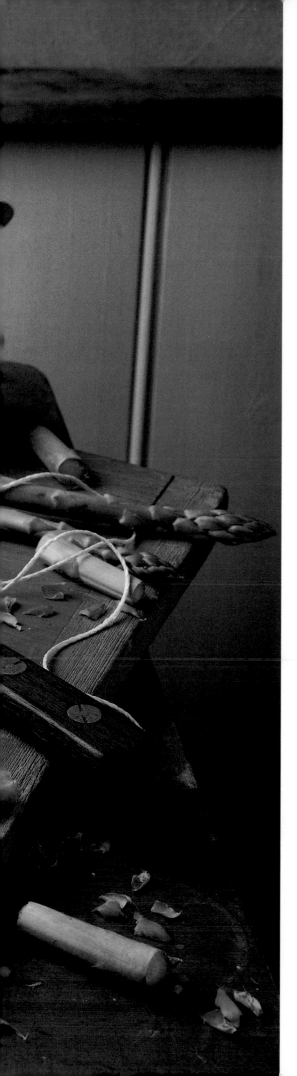

VEGETABLES

*I*t seems extraordinary that even vegetables can undergo a revolution in style, but so it is. From being drab, sink-bound creatures that made a very poor and dowdy appearance on the table, they have become interesting and important. They are now dressed with care and at last have the recognition they deserve. A carefully treated vegetable is very rewarding, offering freshness, colour, flavour and texture. In fact, each individual vegetable has so much character it seems to me quite unnecessary to present four or five different sorts at the same meal. This is a trend started by restaurants, which have to offer a choice, but not a good way to serve them at home.

Putting more emphasis on vegetables means finding interesting ways of dealing with them; of course boiled carrots can be good, but glazed carrots are a great deal better. Vegetables can, in fact, be roasted, braised, gratinéed, scalloped, puréed or fried. So, farewell to the boiled vegetable unless it is worthy of dressing up with no more than a generous dollop of butter.

PERFECT ASPARAGUS (PAGE 110)

PERFECT ASPARAGUS

Bundles of fresh asparagus in the market indicate spring is drawing to a close and summer is not far away. Asparagus is best of all served soon after it is picked, within the hour if you want perfection. In fact, Alexander Plunkett Greene's father went as far as to take a Primus stove into the kitchen garden to cook them within minutes, even seconds, of cutting them with his special asparagus knife. Where his melted butter came from is still a mystery.

SERVES 6

1.5–2 kg (3–4 lb) asparagus
salt
180 g (6 oz) butter

Trim the tough ends off the asparagus, making the stalks all more or less the same length. Scrape away the lower scales, which may be hiding grit.

Rinse well and tie the stalks into as many bundles as there are people, using clean white string.

Bring a large pan of water, large enough to take the aspargus lying down, to the boil. Put in a generous amount of salt, which helps to keep the asparagus green. Lower in the bundles and boil for 12–18 minutes according to size. Test them with a thin skewer to see if they are done, then lift them out by the string. Do not put them in a colander or the tips will break off: drain them on a tilted dish with a cloth on it.

TO SERVE HOT

Serve hot, well drained, with the string removed, on hot plates, and with a jug of drawn butter sauce: bring 2–3 table-spoons of water to the boil in a small pan. Gradually add the butter in little pieces, shaking the pan all the time.

TO SERVE COLD

Or, serve the asparagus cold, with a very good salad dressing, or mayonnaise (see page 159) thinned with single cream, or mixed with lettuce in a salad bowl.

ASPARAGUS READY FOR THE MARKET.

110

BRIGHT GREEN BEANS

There are two schools of thought about the cooking of beans – many home cooks, particularly the older generation, think they should be cooked until they are really tender and soft, by which time they taste delicious but are also the colour of a frog pond.

But a more kindly approach is to cook the beans until they are tender but haven't completely softened and lost their firm texture, and are still a brilliant and beautiful green.

SERVES 4

500 g (1 lb) green beans
salt
butter

*B*ring a very large pan of water to the boil and put in double the usual quantity of salt – say, 2 teaspoons. This will help the beans to keep their colour. Plunge in the topped and tailed beans, sliced if they are runner beans, broken into manageable lengths if they are French, wax, snap or bobby beans.

Let them boil, uncovered, for 8–10 minutes, then test – keep testing every 2 minutes – and when they are tender, but still with a bit of bite to them, drain them immediately and return them to the pan with a good knob of butter. Put them over the lowest possible heat, shake until each bean is glistening with butter, then put them in a heated serving dish and place a nut of butter on top.

BROAD BEANS WITH HAM

Serve this with sausages or as a lunch dish on its own with some crusty bread.

SERVES 4

1 kg (2 lb) fresh broad beans, or 350 g (12 oz) frozen
salt
1 small onion
60 g (2 oz) butter
30 g (1 oz) plain flour
1 glass white wine or stock
60 g (2 oz) cooked ham, chopped
freshly ground black pepper
1 tablespoon chopped fresh parsley
1 teaspoon sugar

*S*hell and rinse the beans, if using fresh. Blanch fresh or frozen beans in boiling salted water for 5 minutes. Drain well.

Chop the onion and soften it in the butter. When it is pale golden brown, stir in the flour and let it simmer in the butter for 2 minutes. Stir in the wine or stock and add the beans and ham, and salt and pepper to taste.

Stew the mixture for 15 minutes, until the beans are tender. Add the chopped parsley and sugar and increase the heat so it boils for a few seconds – do not leave it longer, as broad beans harden if cooked too long.

GARDEN PEAS

Allow 500 g (1 lb) for 2 people (or more), before shelling. Shell the peas and take note, by eating one or two raw ones, as to whether they are young and sweet or elderly and in need of help to make them taste good.

Small, young, sweet, freshly picked peas take about 5 minutes to cook in boiling salted water.

Older peas should be boiled for 15–20 minutes. Taste them after about 10 minutes and if necessary put in 2–3 lumps of sugar. A few spring or silver onions are a good addition to older peas: put them into cold salted water and bring it to the boil before you add the peas. Some people put a mint leaf in the water with the peas.

Serve the peas well drained and tossed in softened butter but not cooked in it.

GLAZED YOUNG CARROTS

This recipe is for the pale-gold early summer carrots sold in bunches complete with their lacy green tops. They look most springlike if the tiniest bit of green top is left on each and the pointed ends of the roots barely trimmed. Avoid buying any wrinkled or 'tired' looking carrots, or any that have brown tips or look slimy.

1 kg (2 lb) young carrots
salt and freshly ground black pepper
60 g (2 oz) butter
1 teaspoon sugar
chopped fresh parsley

*R*emove most of the green tops and scrape but do not peel the carrots. Toss them into a saucepan of fast-boiling lightly salted water and cook gently for about 10 minutes after the water has come back to the boil – very small carrots need even less. They should still be slightly firm. Drain well.

Rinse out the saucepan and melt the butter and sugar over a gentle heat. When you have a pale blonde mixture, put in the carrots and shake them well to coat them with the glaze and cook over a gentle heat for 10 minutes, shaking and turning them frequently. Season with salt and pepper to taste.

Serve sprinkled with chopped parsley. These carrots are delicious with pale delicate meat – chicken or veal – or with grilled fish.

BRAISED RED CABBAGE

SERVES 6–8

1 kg (2 lb) head red cabbage
2 onions
45 g (1½ oz) butter
1–2 tablespoons olive oil
2 apples, preferably russets
3 tablespoons cider vinegar
4–5 tablespoons brown muscovado sugar
dash red wine
1 teaspoon each ground cinnamon, cloves, crushed juniper berries and coriander seeds
1 strip thinly pared orange rind
1 bay leaf
salt and freshly ground black pepper

*Q*uarter the cabbage, removing the central core, and slice it into short strips. Peel and chop the onions.

Heat the butter and olive oil in a large flameproof casserole and soften the onions without letting them brown. Add the cabbage and let it cook gently, stirring occasionally, for about 20 minutes. Preheat the oven to 170°C (325°F, Gas 3).

Core and roughly chop the apples and add them to the pan with the vinegar and sugar and just a dash of red wine – too much liquid makes the cabbage go soft and mushy. Add all the spices and flavourings and cover the pan. Cook in the oven for 1 hour, stirring once or twice and checking to see that it does not dry out. Taste after 1 hour to see if the flavour still has the right balance of sweet and sharp – it tends to lose its piquancy after long cooking, in which case add more vinegar and sugar.

Cook for a further 20–30 minutes, until just tender. Serve drained and hot with all kinds of game or with roast pork.

Red cabbage reheats extremely well and keeps for several days.

BUTTERED CABBAGE

SERVES 4–6

salt
1 head Savoy cabbage or other green cabbage
60 g (2 oz) butter
coarsely ground black pepper

*B*ring a large pan of well-salted water to the boil.

Quarter the cabbage, remove the outer leaves and cut away the central core. Drop the cabbage into the fast boiling water, cover the pan to help it come back to the boil very fast, then remove the lid and turn down the heat a bit. Boil gently for 10–12 minutes, then drain really well for several minutes, cutting through the cabbage in the colander to help the water escape. It should be coarsely chopped.

Return it to the pan and add the butter in little pieces. Heat through, season with coarsely ground pepper if you like it, and if water still comes out, let it simmer gently until it has evaporated, but do not brown the cabbage; it should still be a lovely brilliant green.

BRAISED RED CABBAGE (FRONT); BUTTERED CABBAGE

BRUSSELS SPROUTS WITH CHESTNUTS

This is the dish that Christmas turkey cries out for; it is beautiful, a fresh colour, and has just the right combination of crunch and softness, sweet and rich, that the bland meat of turkey needs.

If you are making this for Christmas, when making the gravy needs your last-minute attention, pre-cook the chestnuts and sprouts and reheat both in butter in a wide pan, giving them an occasional shake or stir to prevent them from browning.

500 g (1 lb) fresh chestnuts, peeled (see page 77), or use vacuum-packed chestnuts
salt
turkey or chicken stock, preferably home-made (see page 20)
500 g (1 lb) Brussels sprouts
60 g (2 oz) butter

*S*immer the chestnuts in a fresh pan of salted turkey or chicken stock for 10–15 minutes or until they are tender; do not overcook or they will fall to pieces. Drain and keep them hot.

Meanwhile, trim the sprouts if using fresh ones, and remove the loose outside leaves; if they are large, cut a small cross in the base of each to speed up the cooking time.

Rinse the sprouts well in a basin of cold, salted water and shake dry. Now plunge them into a large pan of fast boiling water and cook them, uncovered, until just tender, about 12 minutes.

Drain them very thoroughly and add the chestnuts and the butter and toss them over the heat for a few seconds to coat with butter before serving.

CAULIFLOWER CHEESE

SERVES 4

600 ml (1 pint) milk
1 bay leaf
1 small onion
60 g (2 oz) butter
60 g (2 oz) plain flour
salt and freshly ground black pepper
1 large head cauliflower
freshly grated nutmeg
125 g (4 oz) sharp Cheddar cheese, grated
60 g (2 oz) fresh breadcrumbs, toasted
30 g (1 oz) butter

*F*irst, make a really good cheese sauce: heat the milk to boiling point with the bay leaf and sliced onion and let it infuse over a very low heat for 5 minutes before straining it into a measuring jug.

Wipe out the pan, then melt the butter in it. Stir in the flour and let this pale roux cook very gently for 2 minutes, stirring. Remove it from the heat and let cool slightly before adding the hot milk a little at a time, stirring constantly, to make a creamy sauce. Leave to simmer for 15 minutes, stirring occasionally.

Meanwhile, bring a pan of salted water to the boil for the cauliflower.

Cook the cauliflower for 15 minutes, until just tender. Remove it carefully to a colander. Fry the toasted crumbs in melted butter, until crisp and golden.

Preheat the grill. Season the sauce with salt, pepper and nutmeg and stir in the grated cheese.

Place the cauliflower on a flameproof dish, pour the creamy cheese sauce over the top, sprinkle with fried crumbs and place under the grill for a few minutes until bubbling and brown on top.

CAULIFLOWER CHEESE

A VERY GOOD WAY WITH SPINACH

This only takes a very few minutes, is succulent and bright green, and has the most wonderful rich and subtle flavour.

SERVES 6

1 kg (2 lb) young spinach
60–90 g (2–3 oz) butter
salt and freshly ground black pepper
freshly grated nutmeg

Trim and rinse the spinach leaves very thoroughly and drain.

Heat the butter in a very large pan, large enough to hold all the raw spinach. Put in the spinach over a fairly high heat and turn it over with 2 large spoons until it wilts. Season it with salt, pepper and nutmeg. Drain well and serve.

PURÉED SWEDES

SERVES 4–6

1 kg (2 lb) swedes, peeled
salt
60 g (2 oz) butter
at least 75 ml (2½ fl oz) double cream
generous pinch freshly grated nutmeg
very coarsely ground black pepper
(optional)
extra butter or cream, to finish

Cut the swedes into large chunks – if you cut them up too small they absorb too much water. Cook in well-salted water. Drain them well and purée.

If the purée is at all watery, stir over a low heat to evaporate some of the water. Add the butter, cream, salt and nutmeg.

Grind very coarse black pepper over the top if you like it, and finish with a big knob of butter or a swirl of cream.

PREPARING SPINACH

ANY SPINACH BOUGHT LOOSE WILL CONTAIN A GREAT DEAL OF GRIT AND NEEDS THOROUGH RINSING IN SEVERAL CHANGES OF CLEAN WATER, BUT MOST BAGGED SPINACH FROM SUPERMARKETS IS READY TO USE. SMALL, TENDER LEAVES CAN BE USED RAW IN SALADS OR COOKED WITHOUT ANY FURTHER PREPARATION, BUT LARGER LEAVES SHOULD HAVE THEIR TOUGH STALKS TORN OUT. IF COOKING, DO NOT ADD ANY EXTRA WATER TO THE PAN, JUST THE WATER CLINGING TO THE LEAVES IF THEY HAVE BEEN RINSED.

FLAVOURFUL ROOT VEGETABLES — POTATOES, TURNIPS, ONIONS AND SWEDES — ARE A STAPLE OF FINE BRITISH COOKING.

ROAST WINTER VEGETABLES

These vegetables are delicious with roast meat. An alternative way of cooking them is to do them in the roasting tin with the joint or bird. Some people put them straight into the hot fat without any pre-cooking at all but the parsnips and carrots can be rather tough if cooked by this method.

SERVES 6

6–7 tablespoons dripping, see method,
or olive oil and melted butter
6 large carrots
12 small potatoes
3 large parsnips
12 small Jerusalem artichokes
12 small onions
3 turnips
3 kohlrabi
salt

For the best flavour, roast the vegetables in the fat left after roasting a chicken or a piece of pork, as the dripping gives a very good flavour. If, however, you prefer something lighter, use a mixture of olive oil and a little butter. Roast them in the oven with the joint – they take about the same time to cook as a chicken – about 1¼ hours, but they can cook longer without coming to any harm (watch parsnips though, as they tend to burn).

If you are not cooking a joint at the same time, preheat the oven to 190–200°C (375–400°F, Gas 5–6).

Peel all the vegetables, and cut the larger ones into small chunks about the same size as the potatoes. Leave the skinned onions whole.

Bring a large pan of salted water to the boil, drop in the carrots and potatoes and cook for 5 minutes. Then add the rest of the vegetables and cook for 5 minutes

more. Drain very thoroughly. Put the dripping or butter and oil in a roasting tin large enough to take all the vegetables in one layer. Heat the tin in the oven and when the fat is hot, put in all the vegetables and return it to the oven. Baste the vegetables from time to time as they cook and then turn them over with a metal spoon, taking care not to break them. Add more fat if necessary.

When they are golden and tender right through when tested with a skewer, transfer the vegetables to a heated serving dish with a slotted spoon, leaving all the fat behind in the tin.

ROAST ONIONS

These are done in almost exactly the same way as roast potatoes. They are good with roast pork, roast lamb or roast beef. You can make roast shallots in the same way (they take less time to cook, of course) and serve them with lamb chops, pork chops or lamb's kidneys.

500 g (1 lb) onions
salt
30–60 g (1–2 oz) butter and a little oil,
or a few tablespoons of good fresh
dripping from a roast chicken or pork

Preheat the oven to 190°C (375°F, Gas 5). Peel the onions, cutting off as little as possible at the root end, so they stay whole. Put in a pan of salted water, bring to the boil and boil for 10 minutes.

Drain the onions and put into a roasting tin with the melted butter and oil or dripping. Roll them about so they are well coated, and roast them in the oven for 20–25 minutes.

ROAST WINTER VEGETABLES

ONIONS

WHAT VARIETY THERE IS IN THE ONION FAMILY! AS VEGETABLES AND FLAVOURINGS, ONIONS, GARLIC AND LEEKS ARE INDISPENSABLE IN MOST BRITISH KITCHENS. AS WELL AS BEING USED RAW IN SALADS AND DRESSING, MEMBERS OF THIS FAMILY CAN BE BAKED, BOILED, BRAISED, FRIED OR ROASTED, AS IN THE RECIPE RIGHT. THE HIGH SUGAR CONTENT IN ONIONS AND GARLIC IS DISSOLVED BY SLOW COOKING SO THE PUNGENT FLAVOUR EVENTUALLY BECOMES SLIGHTLY SWEET.

GARLIC ONCE RARELY SEEN IN BRITISH KITCHENS, THIS IS NOW A STAPLE FLAVOURING. USE FRESH AND DO NOT FREEZE DISHES CONTAINING GARLIC FOR LONG, AS THEY CAN DEVELOP A MUSTY TASTE.

LEEKS MORE DELICATELY FLAVOURED THAN BULB ONIONS, THESE CAN BE USED IN CASSEROLES, BRAISES AND SOUPS OR ROASTED. RINSE WELL TO REMOVE THE GRIT BETWEEN LAYERS.

RED ONION ORIGINALLY ITALIAN, THESE ARE ATTRACTIVE ADDED RAW TO SALADS, ALTHOUGH THE COLOUR PALES ON COOKING.

SHALLOTS SMALL AND OVAL-SHAPED WITH A RUSSET-BROWN SKIN. IDEAL FOR GLAZING OR ADDING FLAVOUR TO SAUCES.

SPANISH ONIONS DON'T LET THE NAME FOOL YOU. THESE LARGE, ROUND ONIONS ARE GROWN IN BRITAIN AND THEY HAVE A MILD FLAVOUR.

SPRING ONIONS IDEAL FOR USING IN SALADS, THESE LONG, THIN ONIONS ARE HARVESTED BEFORE THE BULBS HAVE CHANCE TO COMPLETELY DEVELOP. SOME PEOPLE DISCARD THE THIN GREEN TOPS BUT THIS IS A WASTE AS THEY HAVE A GOOD FLAVOUR AND CAN BE USED LIKE CHIVES.

FRESHLY HARVESTED WELSH LEEKS READY FOR THE MARKET.

BRAISED LEEKS WITH CREAM

SERVES 6

1 kg (2 lb) leeks
60 g (2 oz) butter
scant 150 ml (¼ pint) chicken stock,
preferably home-made (see page 20)
salt
2–3 tablespoons double cream
coarsely ground black pepper

*T*rim the leeks, removing the coarse green tops and outer layers. If necessary, slit them down the centre to wash out the grit. Slice very, very thinly; they are not going to end up as chunks, but as a soft, green mass.

Melt the butter in a wide shallow pan. Soften the leeks for 5 minutes, stirring them round, then add the stock and a little salt and cook until the liquid evaporates. Add the double cream and a good quantity of pepper, either ground with a pestle and mortar or very coarse from a pepper mill. Simmer until the leeks are bathed in a light creamy sauce, stirring them round to prevent them burning.
Serve hot with grilled beef or lamb.

SEA-KALE WITH TARRAGON

I first became familiar with this under-rated vegetable as a schoolgirl in Suffolk. It grows along the beach, and now some larger supermarkets stock it. If you find any, I suggest you give it a try. It has a delicate, somewhat nutty taste, but goes greenish and tastes like cabbage if exposed to light.

Allow 500 g (1 lb) seakale for 2–3 people. Wash and remove any coarse leaves and discoloured bits.

Tie it into bundles, 1 for each person, and cook it like asparagus (see page 110) in boiling salted water to which you have added a squeeze of lemon. Drain and cover with cream mixed with a little chopped tarragon, or with melted butter, like asparagus with your fingers.

MUSHROOMS IN CREAM

This is best of all when made with country field mushrooms.

SERVES 4

350 g (12 oz) large flat mushrooms
15 g (½ oz) butter, or a little more
salt
freshly ground black pepper
1–2 pinches fresh thyme
150 ml (¼ pint) double cream

*C*lean the mushrooms and cut off the stalks. Heat the butter and gently fry the mushrooms, seasoning them with salt, pepper and a little thyme. When they are beginning to soften, add the cream and cook the mushrooms in it, turning them occasionally with a wooden spoon, until the cream starts to thicken and turns a rich fawn colour.

Serve the mushrooms very hot, either on toast or with bacon, grilled steak or lamb chops.

MUSHROOMS IN CREAM

121

A SCOTTISH FARMER PLOWS HIS MAINCROP
POTATOES.

olive oils in a deep-fat fryer. Lower the basket containing a handful of dry slices of potato into the sizzling hot oil and keep the slices moving about as they fry. When they are pale golden, lift up the basket, increase the heat a little under the pan and then dip them back in until they are a rich golden brown more or less all over. Lift them out, shake well, sprinkle with a little salt and drain on kitchen paper while you cook the next handful, turning the heat down a little to start with.

You can cook these early in the day and reheat them in the oven just before serving. They are exquisite, and perfect, as the name implies, with partridge, pheasant or grouse. If you haven't time to make them yourself – they do take quite a lot of effort – then serve roast potatoes, but never bought potato crisps, which are often suggested as a substitute for game chips.

GAME CHIPS

Buy the largest potatoes you can find, and allow 1 per person. Peel them as thinly as possible and slice them into rounds, again as thinly as possible, by hand or in a food processor. Put the slices into a bowl of cold water for a few minutes, then take out a handful and dry them carefully on a clean tea towel.

Heat a mixture of sunflower and

MASHED POTATOES WITH SPRING ONIONS

SERVES 4–6

1 kg (2 lb) potatoes
salt
1 bunch spring onions
30 g (1 oz) butter
milk
freshly ground black pepper

Peel the potatoes and put them to boil in well-salted water. Skin and trim the spring onions, leaving about 2.5 cm (1 inch) of the tender part of the green tops. Cut them across diagonally into small pieces.

Melt the butter in a shallow pan and put in the chopped spring onions. Add enough water to cover them and simmer until it has just evaporated and the onions are tender and bathed in a velvety, pale green, creamy liquid.

When the potatoes are tender, drain and mash them thoroughly over a low heat; add enough milk to make a soft purée, and give them a really good beating. Add the onions and stir them in; taste for seasoning. Serve piping hot.

SCALLOPED POTATOES

SERVES 6

30 g (1 oz) butter
30 g (1 oz) plain flour
600 ml (1 pint) milk
salt and freshly ground black pepper
freshly grated nutmeg
750 g (1½ lb) potatoes
2–3 tablespoons chopped fresh parsley
30 g (1 oz) Cheddar cheese, grated
a nut of butter

*M*ake a béchamel sauce: melt the butter in a pan, stir in the flour and cook for 1–2 minutes, stirring constantly. Away from the heat, gradually stir in the milk, then return to heat and cook, stirring, until thickened and smooth. Season well with salt, pepper and nutmeg.

Peel the potatoes and slice them thinly, either by hand, on a mandoline, or in a food processor. Butter a 30 cm (12 inch) oval gratin dish and put in a layer of potatoes. Season lightly and cover with a layer of béchamel sauce. Sprinkle with half the parsley. Repeat these layers, then finish with a layer of potatoes, a layer of béchamel and a layer of grated cheese. Dot the top with butter.

The potatoes can either be given a long slow cooking if they are to go in with a roasting joint, or a fast burst in a hot oven. The slow method will need 1¼ hours

at 180°C (350°F, Gas 4). The fast method will need 40–45 minutes at 220°C (425°F, Gas 7). Cover loosely with foil if they look as if they are burning.

WELSH PUNCHNEP

This is a traditional Welsh dish combining potatoes and turnips to make a lovely buttery purée dotted with pools of hot cream.

SERVES 4

500 g (1 lb) potatoes, peeled
500 g (1 lb) young turnips, peeled
60 g (2 oz) butter
salt and freshly ground black pepper
4 tablespoons cream

*B*oil the potatoes and turnips in separate saucepans – this is essential to obtain the authentic flavour. Drain and mash each vegetable separately with 30 g (1 oz) butter.

Combine the 2 purées, season with salt and pepper and beat until you have a light, soft mixture.

Pile the mixture into a heated serving dish and stick the handle of a wooden spoon into the mixture to make 6–8 holes. Fill each with cream and serve hot.

POTATO VARIETIES

I DON'T THINK ANYONE CAN DISPUTE THAT THE POTATO IS BRITAIN'S NUMBER ONE FAVOURITE VEGETABLE. UNBLEMISHED POTATOES ARE SIMPLY QUITE DELICIOUS, OLD OR NEW, WHEN BOILED IN THEIR SKINS. NOT PEELING THE POTATOES ALSO HAS THE ADVANTAGE OF PRESERVING MANY OF THE NUTRIENTS WHICH ARE HIGHLY CONCENTRATED UNDER THE SKINS.

USE THIS GUIDE FOR CHOOSING POTATOES:
BAKING LOOK FOR ALL-ROUNDERS, SUCH AS KERR'S PINK, RECORD, KING EDWARD, CARA AND DESIREE.
CHIPS (SEE PAGE 61) USE DESIREE, MARIS PIPER, CARA AND GOLDEN WONDER.
MASHED POTATOES CHOOSE A FLOURY VARIETY, SUCH AS DUKE OF YORK, KING EDWARD OR GOLDEN WONDER.
SALADS USE A WAXY VARIETY, SUCH AS ULSTER SCEPTRE, MARIS BARD, PENTLAND JAVELIN, ROMANO OR PINK FIR.

WINTER PUDDINGS

*P*uddings, like all the repertoire of home cooks, tend to be seasonal. Winter is the time for comfort, and nothing can be more comforting than sticky steam ginger pudding on a freezing cold, grey day.

We have mentally said farewell to stodge but this does not mean we should throw the baby out with the bath-water. There are some flavours and textures that should not be lost; in my opinion, steamed puddings, for example, come into the category of national treasures, and should always have a place in our cold weather cooking. Bread and butter pudding is another survivor – originally made from the leftover loaf, it has now been glorified by London chefs who bake it in a creamy custard with a light caramelized top. It is a fact not often taken to heart, that something made with inexpensive ordinary ingredients becomes the equal of an extravagant and complicated dish.

RHUBARB PLATE PIE (PAGE 136)

QUEEN OF PUDDINGS

Often dismissed as nursery food, I think this comforting pudding is very much adult food. Use a good quality jam or make your own (see page 168).

SERVES 4

300 ml ($\frac{1}{2}$ pint) milk
30 g (1 oz) butter
grated rind of $\frac{1}{2}$ lemon
90 g (3 oz) fresh breadcrumbs
2 whole eggs, plus 1 extra white
60 g (2 oz) sugar
125 g (4 oz) raspberry or strawberry jam
1–2 tablespoons sugar

*P*reheat the oven to 180°C (350°F, Gas 4).

Put the milk, butter and grated lemon rind into a saucepan and bring the mixture to the boil. Pour it, boiling, over the breadcrumbs and set aside to cool and soak to a creamy mush.

Separate the eggs and beat the yolks into the breadcrumb mixture, together with the sugar. Pour the mixture into a buttered 1 litre (1¾ pint) pie dish, stand it in a roasting tin of hot water. Put in the centre of the oven and bake for 20 minutes. When it has just set, spread the jam over the top – if it is very stiff jam, heat it with 1 teaspoon water to thin it down a bit.

Beat the egg whites to a firm snow. Add 1 tablespoon sugar and beat again. Spoon them over the jam to cover it. Sprinkle with a little sugar and bake for a further 10 minutes, until the meringue is a pretty pale fawn colour.

A WARM AND COSY COUNTRY KITCHEN.

BREAD AND BUTTER PUDDING

SERVES 4

6 small slices day old bread, crusts cut off
butter for the bread
30 g (1 oz) sultanas
300 ml ($\frac{1}{2}$ pint) milk
2 eggs
2–3 tablespoons double cream
4 teaspoons sugar or 3 teaspoons sugar and 1 teaspoon vanilla sugar (see below) plus extra for sprinkling
freshly grated nutmeg

*T*he oven should be fairly low otherwise the custardy part, which should be creamy and delicate, will separate. Preheat the oven to 170°C (325°F, Gas 3).

Butter the slices of bread. Put 3 slices in a 25 cm (10 inch) pie dish, scatter on the sultanas and put the remaining 3 slices on top. Heat the milk.

Beat the eggs, hot milk, cream and sugar together and pour over the bread and butter. Allow to soak for 15 minutes, then bake, covered, for 20 minutes.

Uncover the pudding, sprinkle with sugar and nutmeg and bake for another 20–25 minutes, until just set.

TO MAKE VANILLA SUGAR

Immerse a vanilla pod in a jar of caster or granulated sugar for at least 1 week to give it time to pick up the vanilla flavour. It will then keep happily for months. Refill with fresh sugar as you use it but leave the vanilla in the jar.

LIGHT CHRISTMAS PUDDING

Make this pudding a few days before Christmas or on Christmas Eve if you like, as it needs no maturing. First, and highly important, is the shopping. To make a really good pudding you must buy proper golden Demerara sugar, untreated sun-dried muscatels or jumbo raisins – these are the sticky ones, not the ones you eat with almonds – and untreated sun-dried sultanas. Do not buy currants – you don't need them for this pudding. Also, find whole pieces of candied orange, lemon and citron peels, and buy some of each – do not buy cut peel or, worse still, those boxes of mixed dried fruit. They are just not good enough for this pudding.

You will need ground almonds – I make them myself, buying whole blanched almonds and grinding them a bit coarser than the ones you buy already ground. A food processor does this very well.

On the day you are going to make the pudding, buy or make a loaf of wholemeal bread that has air in it – you must not use a brick-like loaf or the breadcrumbs will not be as light as they should be. You will also need some free-range eggs and a nice lemon (scrub the skin with a little vinegar to remove any preservative from the outside), some Normandy butter, a whole nutmeg, ground cinnamon and mixed spice, brandy and milk.

SERVES 6–8

60 g (2 oz) whole pieces of mixed candied peel (see introduction)

90 g (3 oz) fine fresh wholemeal bread without crusts

250 g (8 oz) large seedless raisins (see introduction)

250 g (8 oz) sultanas (see introduction)

90 g (3 oz) ground almonds (see introduction)

125 g (4 oz) golden Demerara sugar (see introduction)

pinch sea salt

90 g (3 oz) unsalted butter, softened

juice and grated rind of ½ large or 1 small lemon

2 eggs

3 tablespoons brandy

1 tablespoon milk

¼ teaspoon freshly grated nutmeg

½ teaspoon ground cinnamon

½ teaspoon ground mixed spice

*P*our boiling water over the candied peels and let them soak for 3–4 minutes, then drain and cut into slivers. Make fine breadcrumbs with the wholemeal bread. Mix together the raisins, separated from each other with your fingers if necessary, sultanas, candied peels, ground almonds, breadcrumbs, Demerara sugar and salt. Stir or rub the butter into the dry ingredients with your fingertips, until it is well mixed in. Add the grated lemon rind and juice.

Whisk together the eggs, brandy and milk, whisking them well, then add them to the bowl and mix in. Lastly, add the spices, using less or more according to your own taste. Let everyone stir the pudding for good luck, then put the mixture into a buttered 1 litre (1¾ pint) pudding basin. Push in silver charms or a silver sixpence.

Place a disc of buttered greaseproof paper on top of the mixture, cover the basin loosely with a round of kitchen foil and tie it on with a piece of string (see instructions for covering Steak and Kidney Pudding, page 92), making a handle across the top to lift the pudding. Steam in a large, covered pan of boiling water for 4 hours. Top up as necessary with boiling water.

TO SERVE

On Christmas Day itself, steam the pudding for 1 hour and serve with Light Brandy Sauce (see page 160). Don't forget to pour heated brandy over the top and set it alight as the pudding makes its grand entrance at the Christmas table.

JAM ROLY-POLY

This is one of those comfortable old English recipes that have gone somewhat out of fashion today, but are still much loved by many, partly for childhood associations and partly because they are so good and warming. Serve warm with Custard (see page 160) for spooning over each portion.

SERVES 4

250 g (8 oz) self-raising flour
125 g (4 oz) grated suet
pinch salt
300 g (10 oz) raspberry, plum or
strawberry jam

*M*ix the flour, suet and salt in a bowl, and then stir in, with the blade of a knife, just enough water to bind the mixture to a light dough. Roll it out to an oblong shape. Make it fairly thin, about .5 cm (¼ inch). Spread the centre lavishly with jam leaving a 2.5 cm (1 inch) margin all the way down each side and at one end. Roll it up loosely starting from the jammy end, and enclose it in a loose parcel of kitchen foil — it should have pleats in it so that it can expand with the roly poly; this helps to keep the pudding light.

Fill the bottom half of a large steamer or fish kettle with water and bring it to the boil. Put the pudding roll in the top over the boiling water, cover the pan and steam for 2 hours, topping up with more boiling water as necessary. Serve hot.

JAM ROLY-POLY

PANCAKES

Serve the pancakes as you cook them, with slices of lemon and caster sugar, or make a mound of them and keep them hot to serve all at once. If you want to keep them, they can be left to cool, rolled up together and wrapped in foil. They will then keep for a day or two in the refrigerator, and can be filled and reheated in the oven or under the grill.

SERVES 6

150 g (5 oz) plain flour
pinch salt
1 egg
300 ml (½ pint) milk and water mixed
30 g (1 oz) butter, melted
1 teaspoon vegetable oil
extra butter

*P*ut the flour and salt in a large bowl and make a well in the centre. Break in the egg and start stirring it round with a wooden spoon, gradually incorporating the flour. As the mixture becomes thick, add the milk and water gradually, beating all the time. When you have a smooth batter, add the melted butter and beat.

Leave the batter to stand for at least 30 minutes, then beat again.

To make the pancakes, heat a reliable small frying pan, one that you know will not stick. When it is hot put in a little oil and a hazelnut of butter, and swill it round to cover the bottom of the pan.

Now dip into the batter with a ladle and pour in just enough to cover the bottom of the pan. Tip the pan to spread the batter evenly. Let it cook until all the batter is just set — it should be brown underneath, if it isn't the heat is too low. (If it is black the heat is too high.) Now slide a palette knife under the middle and turn it or toss it in the traditional way. Cook the underside briefly.

A TRIFLE*

The prettiest possible decoration for a trifle must be that suggested by Mrs Copley in her *Domestic Cookery* of 1845: 'Stick here and there a delicate flower. Be careful to choose only such as are innocent: violets, heart's ease, polyanthus, primrose, cowslip, geranium, myrtle, verbena, stock, gilliflower (pink) and roses. This will afford a variety and some of them be in season at most times of the year. The trifle is better for being made the day before, but not garnished till the moment of serving.'

SERVES 6

1 Real English Sponge Cake
(see page 182)
4 tablespoons strawberry jam or
Raspberry Jam (see page 168)
125 ml (4 fl oz) sweet white wine
2 tablespoons brandy
freshly grated nutmeg
60 g (2 oz) blanched almonds, split
600 ml (1 pint) home-made Custard
(see page 160)
(*see page 4 for advice on eggs)
300 ml (½ pint) double cream, whipped
and flavoured with sugar, grated lemon
rind and a little brandy
fresh flowers for decoration

*P*ut the sponge cake, spread with jam and cut in pieces, in a trifle dish, jam-side uppermost; a glass bowl is traditional. Pour on the white wine and brandy and let it soak in. Grate a little nutmeg over the top and stick with the almond pieces. Pour on the warm custard and leave it set and cool.

Lastly cover the top with whipped cream, and decorate it with flowers.

Make a marmalade trifle using home-made Seville Orange Marmalade (page 168) instead of jam.

KENT SYLLABUB*

Make this in the morning if it is for lunch, in the afternoon if for dinner. If you keep it longer than an hour or two it tastes better than ever but it eventually tends to separate a little at the bottom. If you do want to keep it, put it in shallow glasses in the coldest part of the refrigerator.

SERVES 4–6

4 egg whites (*see page 4 for advice on eggs)
2 tablespoons caster sugar
300 ml (½ pint) double cream
grated rind and juice of 1 lemon
about 125 ml (4 fl oz) sweet white wine, such as Vouvray or Barsac
thin biscuits, to serve (optional)

*W*hisk the egg whites until they are a firm snow, then whisk in the sugar 1 tablespoon at a time. The meringue should be smooth, shiny and thick.

Whip the cream until it is beginning to thicken, then slowly add the lemon rind and juice, whisking constantly. Then whisk in the wine. The mixture should be thick, soft and smooth, but still pourable. Gradually whisk the cream into the meringue.

Spoon the light, billowy mixture into champagne flutes or other pretty glasses and chill for 1 hour before serving. Serve with thin biscuits, if you like.

CHOCOLATE MOUSSE*

'Mousse' is not strictly an English word but it exactly describes this rich and luscious Victorian pudding.

SERVES 6

3 egg yolks (*see page 4 for advice on eggs)
90 g (3 oz) dark chocolate
60 g (2 oz) sugar
450 ml (¾ pint) double cream

*B*eat the egg yolks thoroughly and put them into the top of a double boiler with the grated chocolate, sugar and 150 ml (¼ pint) of the cream. Stir them over a pan of gently simmering water until the mixture thickens, but take care not to overheat it or it will curdle – the addition of 1 tablespoon of cold milk will prevent this if it looks as if this is about to happen. Leave to cool and chill in the refrigerator until starting to thicken, then whisk with an electric beater until foamy and light.

Whip the remaining cream fairly stiffly and fold it into the chocolate mixture. Spoon the chocolate mixture into a soufflé dish or individual ramekins and chill until ready to serve.

BERKSHIRE BAKED CUSTARD

You can also use this recipe to make a proper custard pie – the sort Laurel and Hardy threw at each other before the invention of shaving cream. See page 187 for instructions for making and precooking the crust, and add the custard at the same time as you would add any other sort of filling. Sprinkle the top with nutmeg and bake at 170°C (325°F, Gas 3) for 40–50 minutes.

SERVES 6

900 ml (1½ pints) creamy milk
grated rind of 1 lemon, or 1 vanilla pod
90–125 g (3–4 oz) caster sugar
1 tablespoon brandy
4 eggs
freshly grated nutmeg

*P*reheat the oven to 170°C (325°F, Gas 3). Heat the milk, lemon rind or vanilla pod, sugar and brandy to boiling point, then remove from the heat.

Beat the eggs lightly without making them froth – it is best to use a fork for this rather than a whisk, or the top of the custard will be bubbly and look as if it is curdled. Pour the hot, but not boiling, milk on to the eggs, stirring constantly with a wooden spoon. Strain through a wire sieve into a 1.2 litre (2 pint) pie dish.

Sprinkle the top with grated nutmeg (or ground coriander or cinnamon) and bake for 50–60 minutes, until set but still tender and wobbly.

Baked custard is lovely on its own or with a dish of stewed greengages or plums, or poached peaches. Eat it sprinkled with sugar.

RICE PUDDING

Where rice pudding is concerned, long and gentle cooking is the order of the day. In the days of kitchen ranges in every kitchen, the tradition was to leave the pudding in overnight with the fires banked down. Nowadays, three or four hours in a low oven will do the trick, turning the rice and milk gradually into a rich, caramel-coloured cream.

SERVES 4–6

60 g (2 oz) pudding rice
600 ml (1 pint) creamy milk
salt
125 g (4 oz) caster sugar
5 cm (2 inch) long piece vanilla pod,
split
15 g (½ oz) butter
freshly grated nutmeg

Preheat the oven to 130°C (275°F, Gas 1).

Butter a 1 litre (1¾ pint) pie dish. Put the rice in the bottom. Heat the milk, with a pinch of salt, the sugar and the vanilla pod, stirring to dissolve the sugar. When it reaches simmering point, remove the vanilla pod and pour the milk over the rice.

Dot the top all over with little slips of butter, grate a sprinkling of nutmeg over the top and set the dish on the middle shelf of the oven. After 30 minutes, stir the pudding. Repeat the stirring every 30 minutes or so until the rice is soft and the milk creamy. Move the pudding to a higher shelf. Bake until a rich brown – it takes 3 hours in all.

KENT SYLLABUB (FRONT); RHUBARB FOOL

RHUBARB FOOL

SERVES 4–6

500 g (1 lb) young, forced rhubarb
250 g (8 oz) sugar
300 ml (½ pint) double cream

*W*ash the rhubarb and trim off the ends and the leaves. Cut it into 2.5 cm (1 inch) pieces and put them in a pan with 2 tablespoons water and 2 tablespoons of the sugar. Heat very slowly, covered, so the rhubarb softens and thins to a purée. Then add the remaining sugar and cook, uncovered, until the purée is thick but soft and a delicate shade of pink. It must not be wet and sloshy. Leave it to get quite cool.

Whip the cream with 2 tablespoons iced water, whisking carefully as it thickens; stop while it is still soft.

Fold the rhubarb purée into the cream, pour it into a serving dish and chill. Serve, if you like, with a little extra cream.

VARIATIONS

Gooseberry fool can be made in the same way as rhubarb, and is less inclined to be wet, so needs less cooking. Raspberries and strawberries are lightly crushed, sweetened and folded fresh and raw into the whipped cream.

When making gooseberry, strawberry, raspberry or rhubarb fools, I do not fold in the fruit too thoroughly; it is prettier and fresher looking to have a rather rough and ready texture, prettily marbled and streaked with cream.

A KITCHEN-GARDEN PLOT OF YOUNG
RHUBARB.

RHUBARB PLATE PIE

What could be simpler than lining a tin pie plate with pastry and filling it with fresh-picked fruit?

SERVES 6

Shortcrust Pastry made with 180 g
(6 oz) plain flour, 90 g (3 oz) butter,
30 g (1 oz) lard and pinch salt (see
page 187)
softened butter
500 g (1 lb) young rhubarb, well rinsed
and cut into pieces
60 g (2 oz) raisins
1 tablespoon plain flour
4 tablespoons sugar
pinch ground ginger
1 egg, beaten with 1 teaspoon water,
for glazing
caster sugar for sprinkling

*P*reheat the oven to 220°C (425°F, Gas 7).

Be sure the pastry rests in the refrigerator for at least 30 minutes before using. Divide the pastry in half. Roll out on a lightly floured surface 2 discs to fit a deep tin plate about 25 cm (10 inches) across. Butter the plate and lay 1 layer of pastry over, pressing it down lightly to exclude air. Brush the bottom with melted butter. Put in the wet rhubarb and the raisins, piling them up.

Mix the flour, sugar and ginger together in a cup and sprinkle over the top of the rhubarb. Wet the edges of the pastry. With a frilly edged biscuit or pastry cutter, cut a hole in the centre of the second disc of pastry. Fold it over the rolling pin and place it on top of the pie with the hole in the centre. Trim the edges and press the 2 layers together with a fork using a criss-cross movement.

Brush the top of the pie with the beaten egg glaze. Bake for 15 minutes to set the pastry, then lower the temperature to 180°C (350°F, Gas 4) and bake for 20 minutes to cook the rhubarb. Sprinkle with caster sugar, and serve hot or cold.

AMBER PUDDING

Despite the name, this Welsh dessert is actually a rich and simple tart subtly flavoured with orange and lemon.

SERVES 6

2 whole eggs, plus 2 egg yolks
90 g (3 oz) sugar
finely grated rind of ½ lemon
2 tablespoons fine-cut marmalade
125 g (4 oz) butter, melted
180 g (6 oz) Shortcrust Pastry (see page 178)

AN OLD-FASHIONED COUNTRY TEA ROOM OFFERING TRADITIONAL AFTERNOON TEA.

*P*reheat the oven to 220°C (425°F, Gas 7).

Beat together the eggs, egg yolks, sugar, lemon rind and marmalade. Beat in the melted butter.

Roll out the pastry on a lightly floured surface and use to line a lightly greased 15 cm (7 inch) tart tin with a removable bottom.

Prick the bottom with a fork, line with crumpled kitchen foil and bake blind for 12 minutes. Lower the oven temperature to 190°C (375°F, Gas 5).

Remove the foil, pour in the filling and bake for 20 minutes, until the top is set. Serve warm or at room temperature.

TREACLE TART

The simplest of traditional tarts, treacle tart is sometimes made with lemon rind or lemon juice to take the edge off the sweetness of the syrup, but it is even nicer and more authentic without, as in this version.

SERVES 6

300 g (10 oz) Shortcrust Pastry made with 180 g (6 oz) plain flour, 90 g (3 oz) butter, 30 g (1 oz) lard (see page 187)
45 g (1½ oz) fresh white breadcrumbs
6 tablespoons golden syrup
1 egg beaten with 1 teaspoon water for glazing

*P*reheat the oven to 220°C (425°F, Gas 7). Divide the pastry in two. Roll out two thirds of the pastry on a lightly floured surface and line a 25 cm (10 inch) pie plate with it. Spread the breadcrumbs over the bottom, then spoon on the golden syrup.

Cut the remaining pastry into thin strips and make a lattice top. Crimp the pie's edge with a fork and your thumb so there is a pattern all round and the lattice is firmly secured.

Brush the pastry with the egg and water glaze. Bake for 12 minutes, then lower the temperature to 180°C (350°F, Gas 4) and bake for 15–20 minutes longer, until the pastry is golden and the filling is set.

Leave for 5 minutes, then serve hot with cream for pouring over each slice.

SUMMER DESSERTS

O ne of the glories of summer is the fruit season; strawberries followed by raspberries, redcurrants and peaches. Another of the season's glories is eating outdoors in the open air. If you can combine the two together then happiness should be yours.

There are two ways of approaching the outdoor feast. First is the back-to-nature approach, standing round an open fire or barbecue and eating with your fingers. For this approach all the dessert that is needed is a large pile of sliced melons and a bowl of cherries or ripe peaches. The other approach is to take the indoors outdoors, and to sit at a table outside with all the usual cutlery and plates. This means proper food, and any fruit pudding, pie, salad, ice cream or sorbet can be eaten in comfort. For an experience of pure pleasure, try a purple fruit salad eaten under the stars.

BROWN BREAD ICE CREAM (PAGE 150), BACK; ROSE PETAL SORBET (PAGE 151)

APPLE PIE

SERVES 6

1.2 kg (2½ lb) cooking apples
juice of ½ lemon
90 g (3 oz) caster or brown sugar
3 cloves
generous pinch freshly pounded
cinnamon stick (or ground cinnamon)
Rough Puff Pastry made with 180 g
(6 oz) plain flour and 180 g (6 oz)
butter (see page 187), or frozen flaky
pastry, thawed
1 egg, beaten, for glaze
caster sugar

Peel, quarter and core the apples, and cut them into slices. Sprinkle them with lemon juice and toss them so they are evenly coated. Put them into a 23 cm (9 inch) deep oval pie dish with a pie funnel in the middle, and sprinkle with sugar. Scatter on the spices. The pie should be neither too sweet nor too sour. If the apples seem particularly unripe, hard or sour, add an extra 30 g (1 oz) sugar.

Preheat the oven to 200°C (400°F, Gas 6). Roll out the pastry. Put a rim of pastry onto the edge of the pie dish, brushing the dish with egg glaze to make it stick. Glaze the pastry rim and lift the remaining pastry into place. Trim and scallop the pie and decorate with pastry leaves. Brush it with egg glaze.

Bake for 10–15 minutes, until the pastry has set, then lower the heat to 160°C (325°F, Gas 3) and bake for a further 25–30 minutes or more. Take it out of the oven and sprinkle the top with caster sugar. Serve with double cream, not whipped, and a bowl of caster sugar on the table.

APPLE PIE (BACK); GREENGAGE CRUMBLE
(PAGE 142)

APPLE VARIETIES

APPLES FLOURISH IN THE BRITISH CLIMATE. THERE ARE MANY HUNDREDS OF HOME-GROWN VARIETIES, BUT ONLY ABOUT 50 AVAILABLE ON A COMMERCIAL SCALE. ALWAYS POPULAR FOR EATING RAW, APPLES ARE ALSO COOKED IN TRADITIONAL DESSERTS AND AS A CLASSIC ACCOMPANIMENT TO MANY ROAST MEATS, AS IN APPLE SAUCE WITH ROAST PORK AND FRIED APPLE RINGS WITH ROAST GOOSE. COOKING APPLES SHOULD BE USED, AS THE NAME IMPLIES, FOR COOKING, WHILE MANY DESSERT APPLES CAN BE ENJOYED RAW OR COOKED. LOOK OUT FOR THESE POPULAR VARIETIES:

BRAMLEY'S SEEDLINGS IDEAL FOR MRS BEETON'S APPLE SNOW (SEE PAGE 147), AS THIS COOKING APPLE QUICKLY REDUCES TO A LIGHT, FLUFFY PUREE.

COX'S ORANGE PIPPIN POPULAR FOR BOTH EATING AND COOKING, THIS JUICY APPLE HAS A LOVELY AROMA.

GOLDEN DELICIOUS ONE OF BRITAIN'S MOST POPULAR APPLE VARIETIES, REFLECTING ITS VERSATILITY AS A DESSERT AND COOKING APPLE. CHEFS LIKE THESE APPLES BECAUSE THEY DO NOT DISCOLOUR.

GRANNY SMITH A GOOD ALL-ROUNDER, EASILY RECOGNIZED BY ITS DARK GREEN SKIN. THIS APPLE HOLDS ITS SHAPE DURING COOK-ING, MAKING IT IDEAL FOR RECIPES SUCH AS APPLE PIE, LEFT, AND ITS TART AND REFRESH-ING FLAVOUR MAKES IT GOOD FOR EATING.

BRAMBLE PIE

SERVES 4

350 g (12 oz) shortcrust pastry, thawed
if frozen
180 g (6 oz) blackberries
1 dessert apple, peeled, cored and
thinly sliced
90 g (3 oz) sugar
1 dessertspoon plain flour
good pinch ground cinnamon
good pinch ground allspice
4–5 cloves
juice of ½ orange
1 egg white
sugar for finishing

*P*reheat the oven to 220°C (425°F,
Gas 7).

*Butter a 20–23 cm (8–9 inch) pie
plate. Roll out half the pastry .3 cm (⅛
inch) thick (keep the rest in the fridge)
and line the plate, trimming the edges
with a sharp knife.*

*Put the blackberries and apple into the
middle. Mix the sugar, flour and spices
and sprinkle them over the top. Spoon on
the orange juice and cover with the
remaining pastry, rolled out to the same
thickness. Trim the edges and crimp them.*

*Make a hole in the centre. Brush the
top with very lightly beaten egg white.
Sprinkle with sugar and bake for 15
minutes, then at 180°C (350°F, Gas 4)
for a further 15–20 minutes, until the
pie is golden.*

GREENGAGE CRUMBLE

SERVES 6

1 kg (2 lb) greengages
180 g (6 oz) caster sugar or brown
sugar
4 teaspoons whisky
90 g (3 oz) plain flour
125 g (4 oz) butter
salt

*P*reheat the oven to 190°C (375°F,
Gas 5).

*Stone the greengages and put them
into an oval pie dish. Sprinkle them with
60 g (2 oz) sugar, 2 teaspoons whisky
and 2–3 tablespoons water.*

*Put the flour, remaining sugar, butter
and pinch of salt into a bowl. Sprinkle
with the remaining 2 teaspoons whisky.
Cut the butter into the flour mixture with
a knife and then rub it in with your
fingertips until the mixture resembles
coarse crumbs. The mixture should be
rough and rather sticky. Spread it over the
greengages as well as you can, but leave it
rough, do not smooth it down.*

*Bake the crumble in the oven for 1
hour, until golden on top. Serve hot with
cream or Custard (page 160).*

SUMMER PUDDING

Summer pudding follows well after a chicken salad on a hot day; it can be made with any soft fruit, but raspberries and red- and/or blackcurrants are the most traditional. Make it a day ahead and cook the fruit lightly with sugar so that there is plenty of juice to soak the bread. A similar pudding is called Paradise Pudding. In this variation, sweet stewed fruit is alternated with layers of bread soaked in milk, ending with a layer of bread, in a glass bowl. The pudding is then covered with a blanket of whipped cream and chilled for several hours.

Summer pudding should be a beautiful deep carmine colour. If the fruit is very juicy, strain off some of the juice, or it will make the bread too wet and it will crumble. There should be just enough to colour it right through. Serve any extra juice separately, or pour it round the pudding at the last minute.

SERVES 6

500 g (1 lb) raspberries
250 g (8 oz) sugar
500 g (1 lb) blackcurrants or redcurrants, or 250 g (8 oz) each
90 g (3 oz) caster sugar
8 slices white bread, crusts removed
double cream, to serve

*M*ake this the day before serving so that the bread becomes thoroughly steeped in the juices.

Cook the raspberries briefly with the sugar until their juice flows. Soften the blackcurrants (and redcurrants if you have them) separately, taking care to let them cook slowly with a little sugar so that they retain their shape.

Line a 1.2 litre (2 pint) pudding basin with the slices of bread, cutting them into shapes that fit together neatly round the bottom and sides. Fill first with redcurrants then with blackcurrants – or with blackcurrants only – and follow with a generous layer of raspberries. Enclose the fruit carefully with more trimmed slices of bread and cover with a plate. Weight the plate with a full bottle or jar. (Do not use a metal weight in case this comes in contact with the juices from the fruit and imparts a metallic flavour.)

Leave in a cool place overnight – not the refrigerator. The next day, turn the pudding carefully out of the basin on to a dish, decorate with bunches of fresh redcurrants and leaves, and serve with thick cream.

SOFT FRUITS

TO ME, THE HIGHLIGHT OF SUMMER IS THE APPEARANCE OF SOFT FRUITS IN MID-JUNE. JUICY, FLAVOURFUL RASPBERRIES, STRAWBERRIES AND GOOSEBERRIES ARE A TREAT ON THEIR OWN AND CAN BE TRANSFORMED INTO THE MOST WONDERFUL DESSERTS WITH NOTHING MORE THAN JUST THICK, RICH CREAM; LUSCIOUS REDCURRANTS AND BLACKCURRANTS NEED ONLY THE SLIGHTEST COOKING. BEST OF ALL ARE BERRIES YOU PICK YOURSELF.

AS WELL AS THE FAMILIAR FAVOURITES, I SUGGEST YOU ALSO LOOK OUT FOR BLUEBERRIES, GROWN PRIMARILY IN DORSET AND SCOTLAND, YELLOW OR WHITE RASPBERRIES FROM SCOTLAND, AND TAYBERRIES, A CROSS OF RASPBERRIES AND BLACKBERRIES, DEVELOPED IN SCOTLAND. SUMMER PUDDING IS AN ANNUAL FAVOURITE BUT IT CAN BE GIVEN A NEW LEASE OF LIFE WITH SOME OF THESE LESS-TRADITIONAL BERRIES.

BROWN BREAD ICE CREAM*

Be sure to eat within a day or two or the crumbs will become soggy.

SERVES 6

2 egg yolks (*see page 4 for advice on eggs)
90g (3 oz) sugar
150 ml (¼ pint) single cream
300 ml (½ pint) double cream
2 teaspoons rum or brandy
125 g (4 oz) fresh brown breadcrumps

*B*eat the egg yolks and sugar in a heatproof bowl until light and frothy. Heat the single cream to simmering point, remove it from the heat, let it cool for 30 seconds, then pour it on to the egg yolks, beating all the time. Put the bowl over a saucepan of simmering water and stir until the mixture starts to thicken. Remove from heat and leave to cool and thicken further.

Whip the double cream until it is soft and light, then flavour it with the rum or brandy. Now fold in the cooled custard with a spatula and lastly the breadcrumbs.

Turn the mixture into a nice-looking container – a soufflé dish is ideal – and freeze. No need to stir. Do not serve this rock hard, but just frozen, otherwise the breadcrumbs may seem too granular.

CRYSTALLIZED ROSE PETALS

TO CRYSTALLIZE ROSE PETALS, PAINT THEM WITH EGG WHITE, LIGHTLY FORKED WITH A PINCH OF SALT (BUT NOT BEATEN). DIP THEM IN CASTER SUGAR AND LEAVE TO DRY FOR 2–3 HOURS ON A RACK.

PEACH ICE CREAM WITH CRYSTALLIZED ROSE PETALS

SERVES 6

1 kg (2 lb) ripe peaches
250 g (8 oz) sugar
grated rind of 1 lemon
150 ml (¼ pint) double cream
crystallized petals (see left), to decorate

*P*our boiling water over the peaches and skin them.

Put them in a saucepan into which they can be fitted side by side, with 600 ml (1 pint) water, the sugar and grated lemon rind. Bring to the boil, then simmer for about 20 minutes or until completely tender, carefully turning them from time to time.

Remove from the heat and leave to cool, then remove the stones from the peaches and put them with their syrup into a blender or food processor and reduce to a purée. When it is completely cold, stir in the cream.

Transfer the mixture to an ice-cream maker or an ice-cube tray and freeze. If you are using a tray in the freezer, beat the ice from time to time as it starts to harden; better still, whizz it in a food processor.

If you like, you can crack the peach stones with nutcrackers, skin the kernels and add them to the ice cream.

Decorate with crystallized pink or peach-coloured rose petals.

ROSE PETAL SORBET*

The most fragrant roses of all are the deep red or crimson musk roses, but any rose with a heavy perfume will make a good sorbet. If you were lucky enough to have masses of Parma violets, you could also make a violet petal sorbet. Rose sorbet should be a very soft pink and have a tiny edge of bitterness from the Campari to cut the sweetness.

SERVES 4

600 ml (1 pint) jug full of rose petals
from very fragrant roses
200 g (7 oz) sugar
2 pared strips lemon rind
juice of ½ lemon
rosewater
2 tablespoons Campari
1 egg white (*see page 4 for advice on eggs)
crystallized petals (see left), to decorate (optional)

*P*ut the rose petals in a big bowl. Dissolve the sugar in 600 ml (1 pint) water over a low heat, add the lemon rind and bring to the boil. Boil for 5 minutes, then pour the liquid over the rose petals. Leave to cool and infuse.

When the syrup is cool, strain it and add the lemon juice, a few drops of rose-water and the Campari.

Lightly beat the egg white and fold it into the syrup. Transfer the mixture to an ice-cream maker or ice cube tray and freeze. If you are using an ice cube tray, tip out the mixture when it is frozen to a slush and whizz it in a food processor or blender, then freeze it again.

You can decorate the sorbet with the crystallized rose petals as described left, if you like.

A GLORIOUS SELECTION OF THE BEST OF
SUMMER FRUITS.

BLACKCURRANT LEAF SORBET*

A similar sorbet can be made with the leaves of rose-geraniums, that good-natured and heavily scented geranium with small, deeply crinkled leaves, or with fresh mint leaves, or with lemon verbena. I have also eaten a sweet thyme sorbet and a marjoram sorbet, very exciting if they are served together with scoops of mint sorbet arranged in a little herbal tri-petalled flower.

SERVES 4

1 lemon
300 g (10 oz) caster sugar
3–4 handfuls young blackcurrant leaves
Champagne or white wine
1 egg white (*see page 4 for advice on eggs)

*P*are the rind of the lemon in thin strips, and put into a pan with the sugar and 600 ml (1 pint) water. Dissolve the sugar over a low heat, then turn up the heat, bring to the boil and boil for 5 minutes without stirring.

Put most of the washed currant leaves in a bowl and pour on the boiling syrup. Leave to cool; the flavour of the leaves permeates the syrup. Strain it when cold.

Squeeze the juice from the lemon and add it with a dash of Champagne to the syrup. Now add the egg white. If you are using a sorbetière for freezing, add the egg white unbeaten; if you are using the freezer, beat the egg white to a soft foam first. Turn the mixture into the sorbetière, or into an ice cube tray, and freeze. If you are using the freezer take out the mixture when it is slushy and whizz it in a food processor or blender, then freeze it again. This will improve the texture and the colour, which becomes paler and more dazzling. To serve, decorate each plate with a couple of blackcurrant leaves.

SAUCES, DRESSINGS AND PRESERVES

*B*ecause supermarket shelves are crammed with row upon row of bottled sauces, dressings, jams and chutneys, it might seem almost perverse to make your own. Not so. If you ever compare the home-made version with its manufactured equivalent, you will immediately see the point of the exercise. It is the genuineness of the home-made which takes it out of the ordinary.

Sauces should be the jewels in any cook's crown. There was a time when the basic white sauce was far from jewel-like. Now, however, we have revised our view of what it should be; light, fresh, creamy, well flavoured and velvety, a delicate vehicle for many flavours. It can enhance vegetables, fish and chicken, provide a basis for gratin dishes and accompany ham.

LEFT TO RIGHT: PICKLED ONIONS (PAGE 164); CURRIED APPLE AND PEPPER CHUTNEY (PAGE 162); PICKLED RED CABBAGE (PAGE 164)

WHITE SAUCE

This plain, easily made, delicious and altogether useful sauce has given rise to a good deal of derisive comment over the years. This certainly should not be so. Here are two versions.

MAKES ABOUT 450 ML (¾ PINT)

WITH COLD MILK

30 g (1 oz) butter
30 g (1 oz) plain flour
450 ml (¾ pint) milk
salt and freshly ground black pepper
extra butter (optional)

WITH HOT MILK

30 g (1 oz) butter
30 g (1 oz) plain flour
450 ml (¾ pint) milk, heated to boiling point
salt and freshly ground black pepper
extra butter (optional)

WHITE SAUCE MADE WITH COLD MILK

Melt the butter in a small, thick saucepan. Stir in the flour and let it cook gently for 1 minute, until it is bubbling. Keep the pan on a moderate heat and gradually stir in the milk a few tablespoons at a time, stirring well after each addition until the milk has been absorbed before adding more. As the sauce becomes smooth and creamy, add the milk in larger quantities. When it is all incorporated, cover the pan and simmer for 15–20 minutes, stirring occasionally, to cook the flour thoroughly.

Now season well and whisk with a wire whisk to obtain a smooth and glossy sauce. A few dabs of butter stirred in at the end give a velvety texture.

WHITE SAUCE MADE WITH HOT MILK

Melt the butter in a small, thick saucepan. Stir in the flour with a wooden spoon and let it cook for 1 minute. Now remove the pan from the heat and allow this roux to cool. Heat the milk to boiling point and pour it on to the cool roux, whisking with a small wire whisk. Don't be alarmed if it does not look smooth at this point. Bring it back to the boil, whisk once or twice and all the soft lumps will disappear. Cover and cook for 15–20 minutes, whisking occasionally and season well with salt and pepper. A few slips of butter whisked in at the end will make the sauce velvety in texture.

The following sauces can be made from a basic white sauce:

EGG SAUCE *(for croquettes and fishcakes)*
Hard-boil 2 eggs for 12 minutes, then cool them under the cold tap, shell them and chop into very small dice. Stir into your white sauce and heat through.

CHEESE SAUCE *(for all sorts of fish and vegetable dishes)*
Grate 60 g (2 oz) of cheese – the ideal mixture is 30 g (1 oz) Cheddar and 30 g (1 oz) Parmesan, but any well-flavoured, dryish cheese will do. Stir the grated cheese into the sauce and beat it well until it melts. Season with cayenne pepper and a touch of nutmeg, but don't put in too much salt as the cheese is salty already.

CAPER SAUCE *(for boiled leg of lamb and fish)*
Make the white sauce; when it is cooked, stir in 1 tablespoon of caper vinegar from the bottle of capers and 2 tablespoons whole capers. Simmer for 5 minutes, stir in 2 tablespoons cream and serve very hot. This is thinner than most of the white sauce based sauces, and is intended to be.

WHOLE DEVON GARLAND CHEESES.

PARSLEY SAUCE

Eat parsley sauce with all kinds of poached fish, including smoked haddock, with fishcakes and with boiled bacon or gammon. It is a very good sauce, and not to be despised or forgotten.

MAKES 600 ML (1 PINT), ENOUGH FOR 6 PEOPLE

600 ml (1 pint) milk
1 bay leaf
1 onion
12 whole black peppercorns
30 g (1 oz) butter
30 g (1 oz) plain flour
salt and freshly ground pepper
3 tablespoons finely chopped fresh
parsley
cream (optional)

*H*eat the milk gently with the bay leaf, peeled, sliced onion and peppercorns, and let it infuse on the side of the stove for at least 10 minutes to absorb the flavours.

Melt the butter in a pan, stir in the flour and let it bubble for 1 minute, then remove from the heat and cool a little. Strain in the hot milk, whisking constantly. Season, return to the heat and stir over medium heat for 5 minutes.

Add the parsley and stir it in for a few minutes, but no longer or it will lose its colour. You can add a dash of cream now if you like. Serve hot.

WATERCRESS SAUCE

This sauce is an interesting alternative to Parsley Sauce (see left), and is rather less well known. Eat with any member of the salmon family, with turbot, brill or halibut, or with boiled gammon or chicken croquettes.

SERVES 4–6

1½ bunches watercress
1 large onion
1 stick celery
450 ml (¾ pint) milk
1 bay leaf
25 g (¾ oz) butter
25 g (¾ oz) plain flour
dash white wine vinegar
3 tablespoons double cream
salt and coarsely ground white pepper

*R*inse the watercress thoroughly, discard the roots and any damaged leaves and chop it. Plunge it into boiling

KITCHEN UTENSILS AT THE READY IN AN OLD-FASHIONED KITCHEN.

water for 1 minute, then drain and refresh under cold water for a few seconds.

Chop the peeled onion and the celery. Heat the milk with the chopped onion and celery and the bay leaf. Let it infuse for 5 minutes.

Melt the butter in a pan, stir in the flour and let it cook gently for 3–4 minutes without browning. Leave it to cool a little, then strain in the milk, away from the heat. Return to the heat and whisk until it thickens; add the wine vinegar, cream and seasoning. Cook for a few minutes and taste it; the basic sauce should taste good in its own right. When you have achieved this, add the chopped blanched watercress. Stir in and cook gently for 2 minutes to bring out the flavour.

CUMBERLAND SAUCE

Serve this traditonal sauce hot or cold with glazed ham, roast venison or cold meat.

MAKES 300 ML (½ PINT)

2 shallots
1 orange
1 lemon
1 piece fresh root ginger, about 2.5 cm (1 inch) square
1 small glass port
250 g (8 oz) redcurrant jelly
salt and cayenne pepper

*P*eel and chop the shallots and cook in a small quantity of boiling water for 2 minutes. Drain.

Pare the orange and lemon rinds thinly and cut into fine matchstick strips. Drop them into a pan of boiling water and blanch for a couple of minutes, then drain. Cut the peeled ginger into fine matchstick strips.

Squeeze the juice from the orange and lemon and put it in a pan with the port, redcurrant jelly, shallots, julienne of orange and lemon and ginger, and a little salt and cayenne.

Cook until smooth and syrupy.

HOT ORANGE SAUCE

This is a classic sauce to serve with duck or wildfowl.

MAKES ABOUT 300 ML (½ PINT)

2 carrots
1 onion
1 stick celery
30 g (1 oz) butter
1 teaspoon sugar
300 ml (½ pint) beef stock, preferably home-made (see page 20)
2 oranges
juice of 1 lemon
1 teaspoon cornflour
salt and freshly ground black pepper
1 tablespoon brandy

*C*hop the vegetables and put them in a thick saucepan with the butter. Sprinkle them with sugar and fry to a deep brown. Add the stock and bring the sauce to the boil. Skim and simmer for 2 minutes.

Meanwhile, pare the oranges with a potato peeler and cut the rind, which should have no pith on it, into small, even shreds. Drop these into a pan of boiling salted water and let them boil for 5 minutes to get rid of their bitter taste. Strain them through a large wire sieve and keep them on one side on a plate.

Now strain the sauce through the same wire sieve, pressing the vegetables with a wooden spoon to extract all their juices.

Return the strained sauce to the saucepan, add the orange and lemon juices, the cornflour stirred into 1–2 tablespoons water, season with salt and pepper and simmer for 5 minutes, stirring all the time.

Now the sauce is almost ready. Keep it hot until the accompanying birds are cooked.

Remove the birds from the oven and put them on a dish. Skim almost all the fat from the roasting tin, pour in the brandy, let it bubble, then pour in the sauce and stir it round until it boils quite fast. Add the shreds of orange rind, pour the sauce into a gravy boat and serve at once.

MINT SAUCE

SERVES 4

3 large handfuls fresh mint leaves
2–3 teaspoons sugar
4 tablespoons wine vinegar

*R*inse and shake the mint leaves, then sprinkle them with sugar and chop rather finely. Put in a bowl.

Heat the vinegar and pour it over the mint. Add more sugar if you think the sauce is too sharp. Serve hot or chilled.

ALTERNATIVE

Use lemon juice instead of vinegar and you can also add a little olive oil. This is not traditional mint sauce, being much less violent in flavour, but it is exceptionally good.

HOT ORANGE SAUCE

FRESH TOMATO SAUCE

MAKES ABOUT 350 ML (12 FL OZ)

500 g (1 lb) fresh tomatoes
1 carrot
1 stick celery
1 onion
1 tablespoon vegetable oil
pinch thyme
pinch sugar
salt and freshly ground black pepper
15 g ($\frac{1}{2}$ oz) butter

*P*ut *the fresh tomatoes in a bowl, pour boiling water over and skin them. Chop the carrot, celery and onion very finely and put them in a saucepan with the oil. Let them cook gently, covered, for 15 minutes, giving them an occasional stir.*

Chop the tomatoes coarsely and put them into the saucepan with the thyme, sugar, and salt and pepper.

Cook the sauce over a medium heat, uncovered, for 15–20 minutes, then purée it either in a blender or with a food mill. Return to the cleaned saucepan and heat through. Stir in the butter and serve.

AN INVITING FAMILY KITCHEN.

CREAMED HORSERADISH SAUCE

SERVES 6

$\frac{1}{2}$ teaspoon prepared mustard
$\frac{1}{2}$ teaspoon sugar
$\frac{1}{2}$ teaspoon tarragon vinegar
2 tablespoons grated horseradish
75 ml ($2\frac{1}{2}$ fl oz) double cream, slightly whipped
pinch salt

*M*ix *the ingredients in the order given, stirring in the cream very lightly. Chill until ready to serve.*

BAKED APPLE SAUCE

This sauce is extremely easily made if you are roasting a duck, goose or a piece of pork. By baking the apples you obtain concentrated flavour.

SERVES 4–6

2 huge Bramleys
4 teaspoons sugar
pinch salt
2 nuts butter

*S*imply *score the skin of the apples all the way round their circumference, and put them into the oven in a dish on the rack alongside or underneath the roasting tin. Let them bake until they are soft right through: test with a skewer and remove them when ready (they will be all puffy with blackened skin).*

Scrape out the cooked soft apple, almost a purée already. Discard the cores. Mix the pulp quickly with sugar, salt and butter and keep hot.

BEST SALAD DRESSING

Salad dressing can be varied according to the type of salad used. A delicately flavoured lettuce heart salad could be made with shallots instead of garlic, lemon juice and perhaps some chopped tarragon or chives in it, while a tougher salad, such as curly endive, needs a good strong dressing with plenty of garlic, wine vinegar and really strong olive oil – if you are not a passionate garlic lover, try rubbing two little pieces of fried bread with a clove of garlic and put them in the bowl underneath the salad.

½–1 clove garlic, depending on the size
salt and plenty of coarsely ground black pepper
1 teaspoon mild Dijon mustard
1 teaspoon sherry vinegar
lemon juice to taste
5 tablespoons virgin olive oil
small pinch sugar, if liked

This can be done very fast if you have all the ingredients on hand. Chop the garlic and then crush it to a fine paste with some salt sprinkled on it.

Put it in a small bowl, mix in the mustard, add the vinegar and lemon juice and then add the oil, gradually whisking it in with a fork or a small whisk so you have a thick emulsion. (If it separates it doesn't really matter, but the emulsified version coats the salad beautifully and doesn't all collect in the bottom of the salad bowl.) Add sugar, if using.

The quantities of garlic or vinegar vary with their strength – some garlic is very mild, some very pungent and vinegar can be vicious or mellow – so always taste the dressing and adjust it if necessary. I have made quite a small quantity, when using larger quantities don't double up on the garlic or it becomes overpowering.

RICH SALAD DRESSING

Avocadoes are not strictly British I'm afraid, but then neither are lemons, a well-established ingredient of salad dressing, nor a host of other things we have happily integrated into our cooking. When they are abundant, I add them to salads on their own, as well as when I make this dressing.

1 small mild onion or shallot
1 small avocado
2–3 teaspoons lemon juice
5 tablespoons olive oil
salt
pinch sugar

Peel and chop the onion or shallot and avocado coarsely and mix in the salad bowl with the other ingredients. Leave in the bottom of the salad bowl and put the salad servers side by side, ends crossed, in the bowl, so that they slightly cover the dressing – this stops the salad leaves from going soggy.

Put whatever you choose for the salad, well washed and dried in a cloth, on top. Mix all together well just before serving.

MAYONNAISE*

To make 300 ml (½ pint), put 2 egg yolks (*see page 4 for advice on eggs) in a bowl and stand the bowl on a damp cloth, so it doesn't slide about. Mix the yolks thoroughly with 1 teaspoon prepared mustard and salt and pepper. Slowly add 300 ml (½ pint) sunflower and olive oils mixed together, little by little, beating in a slow, steady rhythm. Do not try to speed up the process by adding the oil too fast or the mixture will curdle.

As you add more oil the mixture thickens considerably; thin it with 1–2 teaspoons vinegar or lemon juice. Add more oil, in slightly large amounts, but still beating after each addition. Thin with more vinegar or lemon juice as necessary until all the oil is incorporated, then adjust the seasoning. If the mayonnaise is too thick, thin with a little single cream or milk. Serve at once or refrigerate until needed.

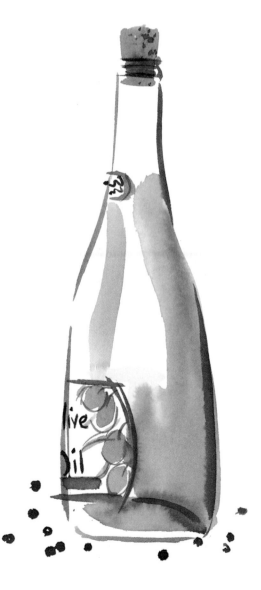

LIGHT BRANDY SAUCE*

When you put this iced sauce on to the hot Christmas pudding on a hot plate, it melts a little to a delicate foam, and gives a good refreshing shock of hot and cold.

SERVES 6

2 egg yolks (*see page 4 for advice on eggs)
2 tablespoons sugar
5–6 tablespoons brandy
250 ml (8 fl oz) whipping cream, chilled, or 150 ml (¼ pint) double cream and 3 tablespoons iced water
1 tablespoon icing sugar
½ tablespoon vanilla sugar (see 126)

*P*ut the egg yolks and sugar in a heatproof bowl which fits over a saucepan. Half-fill the saucepan with water and bring to just below boiling point. Whisk the egg yolks and sugar together away from the heat until they are thick, creamy and pale.

Put the bowl over the hot water, keeping it always just below boiling point, and pour in the brandy. Whisk continuously until the mixture is thick and light; this takes a while, but will happen.

Pour the boiling water out of the saucepan, half-fill it with cold water and put the bowl back; keep whisking the mixture until it is cool.

Put the whipping cream into a large cold bowl and whisk by hand with a balloon whisk or hand beater until it starts to lighten and thicken. Add the icing sugar and vanilla sugar and whisk to a light, but thick, fine foam. Don't overbeat or you will have butter. Fold the brandy mixture into the cream.

Transfer it to a china dish and keep in the freezer until required. The brandy prevents the sauce from freezing too hard.

CUSTARD*

MAKES ABOUT 750 ML (1¼ PINTS)

½ vanilla pod
600 ml (1 pint) milk
4 egg yolks (*see page 4 for advice on eggs)
125 g (4 oz) sugar

*S*plit the vanilla pod and put it into a saucepan with the milk. Heat slowly but don't boil.

Meanwhile, whisk the egg yolks and sugar together until they are pale and creamy. Pour the very hot milk on to the egg and sugar mixture in a slow stream, whisking it in well. Return to the pan and place the pan on a heat diffuser or over a very low heat and cook very gently, stirring all the time. The froth will disappear, and as the custard starts to thicken, so will any large bubbles round the edge.

Remove from the heat when the mixture starts to coat the back of the wooden spoon and strain at once into a bowl. You must never boil custard of this sort as the eggs will curdle instantly, but if a few little lumps form they will disappear when the custard is strained. Serve hot or cold in a pretty jug. This is delicious with Apple Pie (page 141) or Greengage Crumble (page 142).

CUSTARD

CURRIED APPLE AND PEPPER CHUTNEY

MAKES ABOUT 3 KG (6 LB)

250 g (8 oz) raisins
250 g (8 oz) currants
6 firm red tomatoes
6 small onions
3 red peppers
12 eating apples
500 g (1 lb) light brown sugar
1.2 litres (2 pints) distilled or cider
vinegar, preferably spiced (see below)
2 tablespoons whole mustard seeds
2 tablespoons salt
2 teaspoons coriander seeds
1 tablespoon curry powder
1 teaspoon cayenne pepper

SPICED VINEGAR

Heat 1.2 litres (2 pints) distilled or cider vinegar with three 5 cm (2 inch) cinnamon sticks, 2 heaped teaspoons cloves, 10 blades mace, 2 heaped teaspoons allspice berries and 2 teaspoons whole black peppercorns in a covered heatproof basin over a saucepan of simmering water. When the water boils, remove the bowl from the heat, and leave to infuse and cool for 2 hours. Store the vinegar with its the spices in covered bottles, then strain to use.

CHUTNEY

Soak the raisins and currants in warm water for 30 minutes to plump them up. Peel and chop the tomatoes and onions. Remove the seeds from the peppers and shred them into strips. Peel, quarter and core the apples. Combine the sugar, vinegar, spices, salt, curry powder and cayenne in a large heavy saucepan, and bring slowly to the boil, stirring to dissolve the sugar.

Add the tomatoes, onions, peppers, raisins and currants, and simmer gently for 45 minutes. Now add the apples and 2–3 tablespoons water. Bring the mixture slowly back to the boil and simmer, stirring occasionally, until the apples are soft, and the mixture is thick and an appetizing russet colour.

Spoon into sterile glass jars and cover when cool. Leave at least 1 month.

ORANGE CHUTNEY

This is a particularly delicious chutney, dark, rich and hot. It comes from Claire Clifton and Martina Nicolls' *Edible Gifts*. We eat it with curry and with cold poultry and game, particularly turkey or chicken – I also sometimes use it in the sauce when making chicken curry.

MAKES ABOUT 2–2.5 KG (4–5 LB)

4 large oranges
2 large cooking apples
125 g (4 oz) stem ginger in syrup
1 fresh chilli
2 tablespoons currants or sultanas
juice of 1 extra large orange
30 g (1 oz) salt
freshly ground black pepper
350 g (12 oz) soft brown sugar (or less)
3 tablespoons honey
white wine or cider vinegar, to cover

*P*eel the oranges, remove the pith and pips, slice the flesh and finely chop the peel. Peel, core and chop the apples. Drain and chop the ginger. Remove the stem and seeds from the chilli and chop it.

Put the oranges, apples, ginger, chilli, currants, orange juice, salt and pepper into a saucepan. Cover and simmer until the oranges are tender. Add a bit more orange juice if it seems to be drying out.

Add the sugar to taste, honey and enough white wine or cider vinegar to cover the fruit. Mix well and boil gently, stirring occasionally, until it thickens. It will take about 1 hour.

Put into clean warm jars and cap with plastic-lined lids. Keep for at least 1 month to allow the chutney to mature before you eat it.

RED TOMATO CHUTNEY

This is the most delicious chutney in the world, wonderful with cold ham, pheasant or turkey, with pork pie and with all kinds of curry. In fact, the recipe comes from a friend in India, where the tomatoes are really rich and well flavoured. Ours tend to be more watery, so the chutney can take a long time to cook, but it gets there in the end.

MAKES ABOUT 3 KG (6 LB)

2.2 kg (4½ lb) firm, red tomatoes
1 whole head garlic
4 cm (1½ inch) piece fresh root ginger
250 g (8 oz) sugar
1 teaspoon red chilli powder
2 teaspoons salt
2 tablespoons olive oil or mustard oil
4 green chillies
125 g (4 oz) sultanas
½ teaspoon each cumin seeds, brown mustard seeds, fennel seeds and, if available, black onion seeds and fenugreek
150 ml (¼ pint) wine vinegar

*P*ut the tomatoes in a bowl and pour boiling water over them to loosen the skins, then remove the skins and cut the tomatoes into quarters. Put them in a large heavy saucepan. Peel all the cloves from the whole head of garlic, peel and slice the ginger and add both to the tomatoes with the sugar. Add the chilli powder and salt and cook gently until all the liquid has evaporated.

Heat the oil in a frying pan. Cook the chillies, sultanas and spices for a few seconds, then add them with their oil to the tomatoes and mix in well.

Add the vinegar and cook until it is almost evaporated and the chutney has a good, thick consistency. Put in hot jars and cover tightly. Leave to mature for 2 months before eating.

TOMATO KETCHUP

This is only one of the many ketchups or 'catsups' that were the stock-in-trade of Victorian cooks, who used them liberally – all too liberally – to improve their sauces and gravies. But while mushroom ketchup and walnut ketchup have gone the way of the comfortable railway station, where they used to be dispensed from the buffet, tomato ketchup has become the one essential sauce.

MAKES ABOUT 1.4 LITRES (2½ PINTS)

3 kg (6 lb) ripe tomatoes
10 shallots
5 cm (2 inch) piece fresh root ginger, bruised
3 cloves
250 g (8 oz) sugar
1 teaspoon cayenne pepper
2 tablespoons salt
600 ml (1 pint) spiced vinegar (see page 162)
juice of 2 lemons

*Q*uarter the tomatoes and peel and chop the shallots. Put them in a large saucepan and add the bruised ginger and the cloves. Cook until the shallots are tender, then rub through a fine sieve or purée in a food mill, to remove spices and tomato skins and seeds.

Put the pulp back into the rinsed-out pan and add the sugar, cayenne pepper and salt. Cook until the sauce thickens – it takes up to 2 hours – then add the spiced vinegar and lemon juice. Cook again until the sauce reduces to a moist purée.

Pour into sterilized jars or bottles and seal firmly; leave to mature for at least 1 month before use.

APRICOT JAM

MAKES ABOUT 2 KG (4 LB)

625 g (1¼lb) sugar
1.5 kg (3 lb) fresh apricots, half ripe,
half firm

Warm the sugar. Cut the apricots in half and remove the stones. Crack the stones and blanch the kernels in boiling water for 1–2 minutes to remove the skins.

Put the apricots and 150 ml (¼ pint) water in a large pan and stew gently until the fruit is tender, about 30 minutes. Add the heated sugar and stir over a low heat until it dissolves. Then boil rapidly until setting point is reached (see left; it is interesting that an apricot jam that sets straight away and is a clear orange doesn't taste half as delicious as one that has boiled for at least 30 minutes and has become a deeper chestnut colour.) Skim, then stir in the kernels, allow to cool a little before pouring into heated jars.

BRAMBLE JELLY

Pick the blackberries on a dry day. Take a hooked walking stick with you to help pull towards you all those extra fine blackberries that are just out of reach. Also wear wellington boots and trousers. Pick a small proportion of less ripe berries to help the jelly to set. Take them home, pick them over and start cooking them at once.

Put the berries in a deep pan and add 150 ml (¼ pint) water to start them off. Stand the pan in a large pan of water, a sort of deep bain-marie, and put it over a low heat. Leave it for a couple of hours until the juice runs out of the blackberries. Then strain the blackber-

ries through a jelly bag or a cloth. The classic method is to tie the bag or cloth to the legs of the up-turned chair and put the bowl under the jelly bag or cloth. Let the juices drip for several hours or overnight but do not squeeze or the jelly will be cloudy.

Measure the juice and allow 500 g (1 lb) sugar to every 600 ml (1 pint) juice. Put both into a preserving pan, dissolve the sugar by stirring with a wooden spoon over a low heat, then turn up the heat and boil rapidly until setting point is reached (see left). Skim at this point, not before, removing all the froth. Pour into clean, heated jars and cover with waxed paper discs. Allow to cool before covering.

REDCURRANT OR BLACKCURRANT JELLY

Pick the currants on a dry, sunny day. Some people leave the stalks on, but I prefer to remove them for a finer tasting jelly. Do this with a fork, drawing it down each bunch, and the berries will come off very neatly.

Make the jelly by extracting the juice in a bain-marie, in exactly the same way as for Bramble Jelly (left). When you have strained the juice through a jelly bag, without squeezing it at all (see Bramble Jelly, left), measure it and allow 350 g (12 oz) sugar to every 600 ml (1 pint) juice.

Put the juice into the preserving pan and boil for 5 minutes before adding the warmed sugar. Stir until it has all dissolved, then boil for a short time until setting point is reached (see left). Redcurrants set very well and usually reach setting point in a few minutes. Skim and pot as for Bramble Jelly.

TO TEST THE SETTING POINT

TO TEST WHETHER A JELLY OR JAM WILL SET, SPOON A LITTLE ONTO A COLD SAUCER; IT SHOULD START TO SET AS IT COOLS. OR LIFT SOME ON THE WOODEN SPOON AND DROP IT SLOWLY BACK INTO THE PAN; WHEN IT FLAKES OFF THE SPOON, INSTEAD OF RUNNING, IT IS READY TO SET.

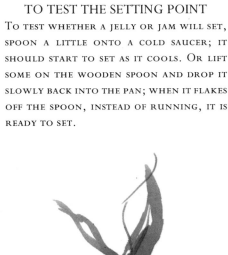

CHRISTMAS MINCEMEAT

This modern recipe gives a very fresh mincemeat, rich without being the least bit cloying or too sweet.

MAKES ABOUT 3 KG (6 LB)

250 g (8 oz) grated suet
500 g (1 lb) sultanas
500 g (1 lb) raisins
1 kg (2 lb) cooking apples, peeled and
chopped

250 g (8 oz) blanched almonds,
chopped
125 g (4 oz) mixed candied peel or
whole citrus peel, cut in pieces
500 g (1 lb) currants
grated rind of 1 lemon
$\frac{1}{4}$ teaspoon freshly grated nutmeg
$\frac{1}{4}$ teaspoon ground cinnamon
$\frac{1}{2}$ teaspoon ground ginger
2 wine glasses brandy

*M*ince the suet, sultanas, raisins, apples, almonds and candied peel

MAKING MINCEMEAT TARTS WITH HOME-MADE CHRISTMAS MINCEMEAT.

coarsely. Mix the fruit together with the other ingredients in a large bowl, but only with half the brandy. Cover and put in a cool place for 3 days, stirring daily, to let the flavours mellow.

Add the remaining brandy. Put in sterilized jars, cover and keep until needed.

167

SEVILLE ORANGE MARMALADE

One of the lovely things about Seville in winter is that the streets are lined with flowering Seville orange trees covered with glowing fruit. This is a recipe given to me by an English friend who lives in Spain and grows her own Sevilles. She lets the peel soak for at least 2 days after its first boiling. Seville oranges are available in February, but they can be frozen until you are in the mood to make the marmalade.

MAKES 3–3.2 KG (6–6½ LB)

1.5 kg (3 lb) Seville oranges
2 kg (4 lb) lump sugar

*W*ash the oranges, cut them in half across and put them in a large pan with 1.8 litres (3 pints) water. Simmer, covered, for 2 hours, bringing the water back to its original level as it boils away. Leave to soak for at least 24 hours. Bring back to the boil, boil for 1 hour and leave to cool.

Remove the orange halves and take out all the pips and pulp, putting them back into the liquid in the pan. Give the liquid and pips one last boil and then sieve, working the pips against the sieve with a wooden spoon to get out all the lovely pulp and as much pectin as possible. Warm the sugar, slice the orange halves thinly and cut the slices across into shortish lengths.

Add the sliced peel to the liquid and heat. Tip in the lump sugar and stir over a low heat until it is dissolved. Then turn up the heat and boil until setting point is reached, 105°C (220°F) on a sugar thermometer (or see page 166).

Skim off any scum, leave to cool a little and pour into clean heated jars. Cover with plastic-lined lids.

LEMON CURD*

MAKES ABOUT 500 G (1 LB)

90 g (3 oz) butter
2 lemons
250 g (8 oz) sugar
2 eggs (*see page 4 for advice on eggs)

*M*elt the butter with the thinly pared rind of 1 lemon in the top of a double boiler over hot water. Stir in the sugar and the strained juice of 2 lemons and heat gently, stirring until the sugar has dissolved. Remove from the water.

Beat the eggs in a bowl, gradually whisk in the butter, sugar and lemon juice mixture and then strain into the top of a double boiler. Stir over moderate heat until the mixture thickens to a cream. Pour into a clean heated jar, and cool before eating. Spread it on bread and butter.

RASPBERRY JAM

MAKES ABOUT 2.5 KG (2 LB)

1.5 kg (3 lb) raspberries
1.5 kg (3 lb) sugar
150 ml (¼ pint) puréed and strained redcurrant juice

*P*ut the raspberries into a preserving pan and bring slowly to the boil. Meanwhile, warm the sugar in a 150°C (300°F, Gas 3) oven. Boil the fruit 2–3 minutes, then add the redcurrant juice and sugar. Stir over low heat until the sugar dissolves, then bring to the boil until setting point is reached (see page 166). Remove from the heat, skim and pour into heated jars. Cover with waxed paper discs, then cool before covering.

A SELECTION OF PRESERVES: SEVILLE ORANGE MARMALADE, RASPBERRY JAM, LEMON CURD AND APRICOT JAM (PAGE 166).

BAKED GOODS

Baking can become something of a passion; making scones or biscuits is a pleasant way to spend an idle afternoon, and kneading bread is positively addictive to some people. It is certainly true that if you bake bread regularly it becomes a satisfying ritual with its own rhythm. It is also very enjoyable experimenting with different combinations of flours and grains to see if you can come up with something that feels and tastes right – exactly the way everybody likes it. Irish soda bread, for example, can become quite individual, unique to each person who makes it. In Ireland it is the pride of every good bed and breakfast, and it can be extremely delicious. When buttermilk is hard to find, an acid milk product such as sour cream or sour milk can be used to activate the raising agent – this can also be applied to scones and any other baking-powder based recipe. It is also better to have the liquid at room temperature.

BRANDY SNAPS (PAGE 185), LEFT; CORNISH GINGER FAIRINGS (PAGE 184)

OLD-FASHIONED POTATO BREAD

This traditional bread has a most delicious flavour and a moist, chewy texture such as bread ought to have.

MAKES 1 LARGE FREE-FORM LOAF OR 2×500 G
(1 LB) LOAVES

500 g (1 lb) floury potatoes
500 g (1 lb) strong plain white bread flour
1½–2 teaspoons salt
15 g (½ oz) easy-blend dried yeast
½ teaspoon sugar
150 ml (¼ pint) milk
15 g (½ oz) butter, melted
extra flour for dusting

*C*ook the potatoes, drain and mash them, then put them through a food mill; keep them warm. They should be dry and fluffy.

Put the flour in a warmed bowl, and mix in the salt, yeast and sugar.

Mix the warm potatoes into the flour. Heat the milk and 150 ml (¼ pint) water to 40–46°C (105–115°F). Add the milk and water and melted butter to the potatoes and flour. Mix to a soft dough and then turn out on to a floured board. Knead for at least 5 minutes, sprinkling more flour on the board as needed.

Put the dough back into the cleaned bowl, cover the top of the bowl with cling film and leave in a warm place to rise. This may take longer than your normal bread, but do not worry, it will come up eventually. When it is 3 times its original volume, punch it down and work for a few seconds, then shape into a big round loaf. Put it on a buttered baking sheet, prick the top here and there with a wooden fork and sprinkle well with flour. Cover with a cloth and leave in a warm place for 40 minutes or until well risen and springy.

Meanwhile, preheat the oven to 190°C (375°F, Gas 5). When the loaf is wobbly when you shake it, put it in the centre of the preheated oven and bake for at least 1 hour or more until it sounds hollow when tapped. Cool on a wire rack.

ONE-RISING BROWN BREAD

Eat this good, wholesome bread as fresh as possible, or freeze it. It doesn't keep quite as well as two-rising brown loaves, but it is exceptionally quick to make and very good. Use fresh yeast if you can; dried yeast seems to take longer and doesn't, in this case, give such good results.

MAKES 3×500 G (1 LB) LOAVES

750 g (1½ lb) Granary flour
750 g (1½ lb) stoneground wholemeal flour
3 teaspoons salt (optional)
60 g (2 oz) butter
45 g (1½ oz) fresh yeast
1 teaspoon honey
1 tablespoon molasses

*C*ombine the flours, then put 1.2 kg (2¾ lb) flour and the salt into a large bowl, rub in the butter and leave in a warm place.

Mix the yeast into 300 ml (½ pint) lukewarm water, add the honey and leave in a warm place for 10 minutes to froth up. Dissolve the molasses in 600 ml (1 pint) lukewarm water.

Make a well in the centre of the flour and pour in the liquids. Stir it all together and then start to knead the dough with your hands. When it forms a cohesive mass in the bowl, flour a work surface and tip out the dough.

Knead it for 5 minutes, slowly adding more flour as it is needed. You may end up with about 125 g (4 oz) flour left over. Divide the dough, which should be very light and springy, into 3 pieces. Form into loaves by making a flat oval and then rolling this up. Tuck the ends of each roll underneath and lower them into well-buttered tins. Cover with a cloth and leave to rise in a warm place (not too hot), or until double in size and springy.

Meanwhile, preheat the oven to 200°C (400°F, Gas 6). Bake the loaves for 40 minutes. Cool on a wire rack.

BROWN SODA BREAD

MAKES 1 LOAF

350 g (12 oz) plain wholemeal flour
125 g (4 oz) plain white flour
1 teaspoon bicarbonate of soda
1 teaspoon cream of tartar
1½ teaspoons salt
30 g (1 oz) butter
300 ml (½ pint) buttermilk or sour milk

*P*reheat the oven to 225°C (425°F, Gas 7).

Combine the flours, bicarbonate of soda, cream of tartar and salt. Rub in the butter. Pour the buttermilk into the flour and knead on a floured board for a few minutes.

Shape into a flattened round and cut a cross right across the middle. Sprinkle the top lightly with flour and place carefully on a greased baking sheet. Bake for 30–40 minutes, until golden and just cooked through – test with a skewer.

Remove to a rack, cover the loaf lightly with a slightly damp cloth and allow to cool. Eat sliced, with butter, preferably the same day as it is made.

BROWN SODA BREAD (LEFT AND FRONT);
ONE-RISING BROWN BREAD

IRISH FRUIT BREAD

This is a good breakfast bread and keeps well, if uncut, for up to 4 days.

MAKES 3×1 KG (2 LB) LOAVES

250 g (8 oz) butter or lard
1 kg (2 lb) strong white bread flour
45 g (1½ oz) fresh yeast
300 ml (½ pint) milk, warm
250 g (8 oz) raisins or sultanas
60 g (2 oz) candied peel, shredded
180 g (6 oz) soft brown sugar
½ nutmeg, grated
large pinch ground mixed spice
½ teaspoon salt
2 eggs

Put the butter and flour in a slightly warmed bowl. Rub the butter into the flour as if you were starting to make pastry. Mix the yeast with a little of the measured amount of warm milk and pour it into a well in the centre of the flour. Flick flour over, stand the bowl in a warm place and wait until the yeast froths and cracks the flour.

Add the fruit, sugar, spices and salt and the eggs beaten with some of the milk, then mix everything together, adding more milk as needed. Knead into a smooth and resilient dough and leave to rise for 2 hours or longer, even overnight, in a warm kitchen. Knock down the dough, divide it and push it into greased loaf tins, pressing it down well. Leave to prove for 30 minutes, or until doubled in size. Meanwhile, preheat the oven to 220°C (425°F, Gas 7).

Bake for 15 minutes, take the loaves out, brush them with top of the milk, turn them round and put them back to bake for a further 30–35 minutes at 190°C (375°F, Gas 5).

Cool the loaves on a wire rack and keep in covered tins.

CHEESE SCONES

MAKES 12

250 g (8 oz) plain flour
1 teaspoon bicarbonate of soda
1 teaspoon cream of tartar
pinch salt
60 g (2 oz) butter
60 g (2 oz) cheese, such as Cheddar, grated
125 ml (4 fl oz) buttermilk or sour milk

Preheat the oven to 190°C (375°F, Gas 5).

Sieve the flour, bicarbonate of soda, cream of tartar and salt into a bowl.

Rub in the butter and stir in the grated cheese, then make the mixture into a light dough with buttermilk or sour milk.

Roll out 1 cm (½ inch) thick on a floured board. Cut into rounds, dust the tops with flour and bake for 20 minutes. Cool on wire racks.

CHEESE SCONES (LEFT); YORKSHIRE BUNS (PAGE 176)

BRAMBLE SCONES

This is a lovely autumn recipe, particularly useful in the country when you have been out walking and picked a few handfuls of blackberries, but not enough to make jam or jelly. These scones look wonderfully home-made.

MAKES 6–8

125 g (4 oz) plain flour
2 teaspoons baking powder
1 tablespoon caster sugar
60 g (2 oz) butter, diced
60 g (2 oz) blackberries, very ripe
2 tablespoons single or soured cream
milk and sugar for glazing

*P*reheat the oven to 200°C (400°F, Gas 6). Sieve the flour, baking powder and sugar into a bowl, rub in the butter with your fingers until it looks like coarse crumbs, then drop in the blackberries.

Mix the cream in with your fingers, adding a little more if necessary to make a light, soft dough. Work lightly – the less it is handled the better. Roll the dough out lightly 1 cm (½ inch) thick and cut into 6 cm (2½ inch) circles. Brush with milk, sprinkle with coarse sugar, place on a buttered and floured baking sheet and bake for 10–15 minutes.

Eat the scones while they are still warm, buttered. You can use well-drained frozen blackberries instead of fresh – they are very good, too.

YORKSHIRE BUNS

Eat these fresh. Mrs Millson, a Yorkshire lady who gave me this recipe, says they should be eaten as they are, not split and buttered. They are to eat with coffee.

MAKES 10–12

250 g (8 oz) plain flour
2½ teaspoons baking powder
125 g (4 oz) Demerara sugar
60 g (2 oz) best plump sultanas, or raisins
125 g (4 oz) butter at room temperature
1 egg, size 1, or 2 eggs, size 3

*P*reheat the oven to 180°C (350°F, Gas 4). Sieve the flour and baking powder and mix well in a bowl with the sugar and sultanas. Add the butter and well-beaten eggs and work everything together lightly with your hands to make a soft paste.

Roll the paste out gently on a floured board to about 1 cm (½ inch) thick and cut into 6 cm (2½ inch) rounds with a plain cutter or a wine glass. Place on a baking sheet and bake in the top of the oven for 10 minutes – do not overbrown, they should be tan coloured.

Eat the buns as soon as they are cool; they are wonderfully light, crisp outside and soft inside.

DROP SCONES OR SCOTCH PANCAKES

These small soft pancakes are very quick to make. I have tried many different methods; the best are made with plain flour, as here, bicarbonate of soda and cream of tartar, not with baking powder nor with self-raising flour. I like them plain, fresh and warm, served with butter and honey or jam.

MAKES 16–20

200 g (7 oz) plain flour
½ teaspoon bicarbonate of soda
1 teaspoon cream of tartar
¼ teaspoon salt
pinch sugar (optional)
2 eggs
300 ml (½ pint) milk or a little less
lard for frying

*S*ieve the flour, bicarbonate of soda, cream of tartar, salt and sugar into a bowl. Beat the eggs and stir them into the flour, gradually beating in the milk until you have a thickish, creamy batter.

Grease a griddle or a heavy iron frying pan lightly with lard and heat it until it is faintly smoking. Drop tablespoons of the mixture on to the griddle or pan, and when fairly large bubbles start to rise to the surface, flip the pancakes over carefully with a spatula. They should be well risen, nicely marked like tortoiseshell and a golden brown on both sides. Serve hot.

AFTERNOON TEA READY FOR SERVING.

CRUMPETS

Crumpets are a lovely thing to serve for tea in the dreaded dark afternoons of winter, best of all toasted in front of a fire, on a toasting fork. They take a bit of practice to get right.

MAKES 8–10

150 ml (¼ pint) milk
15 g (½ oz) unsalted butter
1 teaspoon easy-blend dried yeast or
15 g (½ oz) fresh yeast
1 teaspoon sugar
250 g (8 oz) strong plain white bread flour
¾ teaspoon salt
½ teaspoon baking powder

*H*eat the milk and butter in a small saucepan. When the liquid comes to the boil remove from the heat and add 4 tablespoons water. Let the mixture cool to just over blood heat, 40°C (105°F) for fresh yeast or 46°C (115°F) for dried.

Put the easy-blend yeast or crumbled fresh yeast, sugar, flour and salt in a warmed bowl and beat in the liquid with a wooden spoon. When you have a smooth batter, cover the bowl and leave in a warm place to rise for about 1 hour, until at least twice the volume.

Dissolve the baking powder in 3 tablespoons warm water and stir it into the mixture. Let it rise for 20 minutes.

Grease three 7.5 cm (3 inch) crumpet rings with handles and arrange them on a greased griddle. Heat the griddle and spoon 2 tablespoons of the mixture into each ring. Cook until bubbles rise and set on the top, then lift off the rings, turn the crumpets over and cook for 2–3 minutes more, or until lightly browned. Always put the batter into heated rings or it will stick. Cool on a rack. To serve, toast on both sides and butter well.

WELSH CAKES

MAKES 10–12

250 g (8 oz) plain flour
pinch salt
90 g (3 oz) sugar
½ teaspoon ground mace
¼ teaspoon bicarbonate of soda
¼ teaspoon cream of tartar
60 g (2 oz) butter
30–60 g (1–2 oz) lard
90 g (3 oz) sultanas or currants
1 egg, well beaten
a little milk

*S*ieve the flour, salt, sugar, mace, bicarbonate of soda and cream of tartar together into a bowl. Rub in the butter and lard until the mixture resembles breadcrumbs. Stir in the sultanas or currants and then add beaten egg and enough milk to make a light dough.

Roll out fairly thinly on a floured surface and cut out 5 cm (2 inch) rounds.

Heat the griddle or frying pan until it feels comfortably hot if you hold your hand about 2.5 cm (1 inch) above the surface. Rub the surface of the heated griddle with a piece of paper dipped into lard. Cook gently for 5–6 minutes on each side. Eat warm and buttered.

TEACAKES

These can be served for tea or breakfast, but should always be warm. If you like toasted teacakes, toast the cut sides only.

MAKES 10–12

30 g (1 oz) fresh yeast, or 15 g (½ oz) easy-blend dried yeast
¼ teaspoon sugar
1 kg (2 lb) plain flour
1 tablespoon salt
60 g (2 oz) butter
few currants or sultanas (optional)
1 egg, beaten
150 ml (¼ pint) milk, warm

*P*ut the crumbled fresh yeast or dried easy-blend yeast, sugar, flour and salt in a large bowl and rub in the butter with your fingertips. Add the currants or sultanas at this point if you want to include them. Make a well in the centre of the flour and add the beaten egg, warm milk and as much warm water as is needed to make a soft, pliable dough – about 300 ml (½ pint).

Put the mass of dough on a floured worktop, cover it with a cloth and let it rest whilst you wash out the bowl. This allows the flour to absorb the liquid thoroughly, making the dough easier to handle.

Now knead the dough thoroughly for 5–10 minutes, until it is silky smooth. Put it back into the bowl, cover the top of the bowl with cling film and put a folded tea towel on top to hold in the warmth. Leave it to rise in a warm kitchen for 2–3 hours or until it is more than double in size.

Punch down the dough, then take 125 g (4 oz) lumps at a time and shape them into round, flat cakes about 10 or 12.5 cm (4 or 5 inches) across. Dust lightly with flour. Cover loosely with a tea towel and leave to prove on greased baking sheets.

Meanwhile, preheat the oven to 180–190°C (350–375°F, Gas 4–5). When the teacakes have become soft and slightly puffy, bake them for 30–35 minutes.

Split in half while still warm, butter and then cut in quarters.

MADEIRA CAKE

This is a very good, plain, moist cake, excellent in the middle of the morning with a glass of wine or with coffee.

SERVES 6

150 g (5 oz) plain flour
30 g (1 oz) cornflour
1 teaspoon baking powder
pinch salt
125 g (4 oz) butter, softened
150 g (5 oz) sugar
2 eggs
2 tablespoons milk
citron peel, or whole crystallized lemon or orange peel

*P*reheat the oven to 180°C (350°F, Gas 4). Sieve together the flour, cornflour, baking powder and salt. Cream the butter and sugar together until they are pale and light. Add 1 egg, beat it in, then add half the flour and beat it in; add the remaining egg and flour alternately. Finally, beat in the milk.

Turn the mixture into a buttered and floured 13 cm (5 inch) cake tin. Bake in the middle of the oven for 1¼ hours; after 30 minutes decorate the top of the cake with a few pieces of citron peel. Cool on a wire rack.

WALNUT CAKE*

Fuller's tearooms used to be the place for an afternoon tea. The highspot of tea was the walnut cake, moist yet crumbly, with thick snow-white icing with halved walnuts on top.

SERVES 6

1 tablespoon plain flour
1 tablespoon sugar
125 g (4 oz) unsalted butter
125 g (4 oz) caster sugar
2 eggs
125 g (4 oz) self-raising flour
45 g (1½ oz) walnuts, coarsely ground
handful of walnut halves

ICING

1 egg white (*see page 4 for advice on eggs)
pinch salt
180 g (6 oz) icing sugar, sifted
1 teaspoon double cream

*P*reheat the oven to 180°C (350°F, Gas 4). Butter and flour a deep 15 cm (6 inch) cake tin.

Cream the butter and sugar until light and fluffy. Add the eggs 1 at a time, beating the first one in very well before you add the second. Add the flour and the coarsely ground walnuts. Mix well together for a few seconds and turn into the prepared tin. Bake for 1 hour.

Meanwhile, make the icing. Beat the egg white until stiff with an electric beater. Add the salt and then the icing sugar, still beating. When the mixture is soft and thick and stands up in peaks beat in the cream.

Leave the cake to set for a few minutes before turning out to cool on a rack. When cool, ice and decorate. Spread the icing over the cake. Decorate with a circle of walnuts and leave for at least 4 hours.

DUNDEE CAKE

The ground almonds make this a delicious cake, and one that keeps well in an air-tight container. Make it the day before you want to eat.

SERVES 6–8

125 g (4 oz) currants
125 g (4 oz) sultanas
125 g (4 oz) raisins
125 g (4 oz) glacé cherries, halved
150 g (5 oz) plain flour, plus extra for tin
125 g (4 oz) ground almonds
pinch salt
180 g (6 oz) butter, softened
180 g (6 oz) muscovado or other soft dark brown sugar
3 eggs, size 1
1 tablespoon whisky
12 whole blanched almonds for decorating the top

*P*reheat the oven to 170°C (325°F, Gas 3). Toss the currants, sultanas, raisins and cherries in 30 g (1 oz) of the flour. Mix the remaining flour, ground almonds and salt in a large bowl.

Cream together the butter and sugar and beat the eggs. Add the flour mixture and eggs alternately to the butter and sugar mixture, working them in lightly with a wooden spoon. Gently blend in the whisky. Fold in the fruits so they are evenly distributed.

Line a deep 15 cm (6 inch) cake tin with buttered greaseproof paper and flour it. Turn the mixture into the tin and decorate the top with a ring of almonds.

Bake for 1¾–2 hours, covering lightly with foil when the top looks cooked and the almonds light brown. Test with a skewer to see if the cake is done.

Allow to cool in the tin and keep overnight before cutting.

A CLEVER WAY TO STORE AND DISPLAY A FAMILY'S CUTLERY.

MUSSELBURGH GINGERBREAD CAKE

SERVES 8

I based this cake on an original recipe in Dorothy Allhusen's lovely *Book of Scents and Dishes* written in 1926, in which she gives the names of all the friends whose recipes she publishes. In this case the originator was the Lord Elphinstone of Carberry Tower, Musselburgh. He must have been a gourmet.

350 g (12 oz) plain flour
30 g (1 oz) ground ginger
pinch ground mixed spice
pinch salt
250 g (8 oz) soft margarine
125 g (4 oz) black treacle
125 g (4 oz) golden syrup
4 eggs
125 g (4 oz) muscovado sugar
60 g (2 oz) whole candied orange peel, chopped

*P*reheat the oven to 180°C (350°F, Gas 4). Butter and flour a shallow 23 cm (9 inch) round cake tin or a 20 cm (8 inch) square tin.

Sift the flour, ginger and mixed spice in a bowl, with a pinch of salt. Work the margarine, treacle and syrup together in a bowl until they are smoothly blended. Beat the eggs and sugar together well, then stir in the treacle mixture and the chopped orange peel. Fold in the spiced flour.

Put the mixture into the prepared tin. Bake for 1 hour, covering lightly with foil after 30 minutes to prevent the top from darkening or becoming tough.

Allow to cool and settle overnight before cutting. Keep wrapped in foil to prevent it from drying out.

REAL ENGLISH SPONGE CAKE

A real sponge contains no butter, and was originally made with eight or so eggs, which provided the necessary air and lightness. One Victorian recipe for a rich sponge calls for 16 eggs. Nowadays, people use fewer eggs and self-raising flour to obtain a light cake, so this Edwardian recipe is more useful.

SERVES 6–8

1 tablespoon plain flour
1 tablespoon sugar
150 g (5 oz) caster sugar
4 eggs
grated rind of ½ lemon
150 g (5 oz) self-raising flour
jam and whipped cream to finish

*P*reheat the oven to 200°C (400°F, Gas 6). Mix the plain flour and 1 tablespoon sugar together. Butter two 18 cm (7 inch) sponge or sandwich tins and sprinkle them thickly with the flour and sugar mixture.

Moisten the caster sugar with 2 table-

CHERRY CAKE (LEFT AND BACK); SHORTBREAD (PAGE)

spoons boiling water. Let it cool. Beat the eggs and sugar for about 5 minutes until creamy. Stir in the lemon rind.

Now stir the flour into the egg and sugar mixture by hand. Turn into the sponge tins and bake for 20–25 minutes, until nicely crusted. Leave to shrink from the sides of the tins, then turn out on to racks. Cool slowly in a warm place.

Spread the lower half with jam and the upper half with unsweetened whipped cream. Sandwich together.

CHERRY CAKE

Like the Dark Chocolate Cake (see right), this is a wide shallow cake, easy to cut into small slices to tempt people who normally wouldn't eat a piece of cake, or into large slices for people who love cake.

SERVES 10–12

500 g (1 lb) glacé cherries
270 g (9 oz) soft margarine
300 g (10 oz) caster sugar
grated rind of 1 large lemon
5 eggs, separated
150 g (5 oz) self-raising flour, plus a little extra
icing sugar, to decorate

*B*utter a 32 cm (12½ inch) flan tin and preheat the oven to 180°C (350°F, Gas 4).

Put the cherries in a sieve and steam them over a pan of boiling water to remove excess syrup. Then dry them in a cloth and toss them in a little flour.

Cream the margarine and sugar together in a bowl. Add the grated lemon rind. Whisk the egg yolks and stir them into the egg and sugar mixture. Sieve in the flour and fold it in, then fold in the cherries.

Whisk the egg whites until they form stiff peaks and fold them into the mixture. Fill the tin and bake for 35–40 minutes. Leave to cool and dust with icing sugar. It should not be completely cooked, as it is nicer slightly gooey, and keeps very well.

DARK CHOCOLATE CAKE

Make this in a 32 cm (12½ inch) flan tin with a removable base. The idea is that it is a wide shallow cake, rather than a small deep one. It's much easier to serve and eat as it doesn't tip over on the plate and every slice has a very generous amount of icing. The cake is meant to be fudgey and not, like so many horrible modern cakes, all airy and fluffy and dry. If you haven't got a large enough cake tin, use a small baking tin lined with foil.

SERVES 10–12

265 g (8½ oz) dark chocolate – the darker the better
265 g (8½ oz) caster sugar
190 g (6½ oz) butter, softened
6 eggs, separated
6 tablespoons self-raising flour

ICING
190 g (6½ oz) dark chocolate
10 sugar lumps dissolved in a little black coffee
60 g (2 oz) butter, cut up

*B*utter the tin and preheat the oven to 200°C (400°F, Gas 6).

Melt the chocolate. Beat the sugar, butter and egg yolks to a cream, and stir in the chocolate.

Sieve the flour and fold it in and lastly whisk the egg whites to a firm snow and fold them in. Transfer the mixture to the tin and bake for 30–35 minutes. Remove the outer ring of the tin and leave the cake to cool.

To make the icing, melt the chocolate in the top of a double boiler with the sugar and coffee. Stir in the butter, beating until smooth.

Spread the icing over the cake with a palette knife while it is still warm.

BAKING CAKES

SADLY, HOME-MADE CAKES ARE BECOMING LESS OF AN OCCURRENCE THAN THEY ONCE WERE. YET, FEW BAKED GOODS ARE MORE WELCOMED AND APPRECIATED. I ENJOY BAKING CAKES BUT I KNOW IT CAN BE DIFFICULT TO GET A SUCCESSFUL RESULT. HERE ARE SOME COMMON PROBLEMS AND THEIR POSSIBLE CAUSES:

CRUSTY TOP THIS INDICATES TOO MUCH SUGAR IN THE MIXTURE.

DENSE, HEAVY CAKE THE MIXTURE COULD HAVE BEEN OVER-BEATEN, OR THERE WAS NOT ENOUGH RAISING AGENT.

PEAKED TOP TOO MUCH RAISING AGENT IN THE MIXTURE IS THE MOST LIKELY CAUSE, BUT PEAKED TOPS CAN ALSO BE CAUSED BY TOO HIGH A TEMPERATURE.

SUNKEN CENTRE THE MOST COMMON CAUSES ARE OPENING THE OVEN DOOR SOONER THAN HALFWAY THROUGH THE BAKING TIME, CREATING A DRAUGHT, OR THAT THE OVEN TEMPERATURE WAS TOO LOW. OTHER CAUSES INCLUDE TOO MUCH LIQUID OR NOT ENOUGH BAKING TIME.

ROCK CAKES

Surely nobody but the British could give something as delicious as these quickly made little mounds of sugary, curranty crumble a title as prosaic as 'rock cakes'; but eat them the day they are made or they will begin to earn the name.

MAKES 20–24

125 g (4 oz) butter, softened
125 g (4 oz) Demerara sugar
250 g (8 oz) self-raising flour
180 g (6 oz) sultanas and currants mixed
60 g (2 oz) candied peel, chopped
1 egg
150 ml (¼ pint) milk

Grease and flour 2 baking sheets and preheat the oven to 190°C (375°F, Gas 5).

Cream butter and sugar briefly, add the remaining ingredients, mix well and heap in little rough mounds on the baking sheets. Bake for 15–20 minutes. Cool on wire racks.

CORNISH GINGER FAIRINGS

These gingery biscuits used to be sold at fairs and eaten with spiced ale.

MAKES 25

250 g (8 oz) plain flour
2 teaspoons baking powder
2 teaspoons ground ginger
½ teaspoon ground mixed spice
½ teaspoon ground cinnamon
grated lemon rind (optional)
125 g (4 oz) margarine
125 g (4 oz) sugar
3 tablespoons golden syrup

Preheat the oven to 190°C (375°F, Gas 5).

Mix all the dry ingredients together except the sugar. Rub in the margarine and then stir in the sugar.

Heat the syrup until it runs and add to the mixture. Shape and roll into balls the size of a walnut, place these on a greased baking sheet on the top shelf of the oven. When the biscuits begin to colour, after 10–15 minutes, remove the baking sheet, bang it sharply on the table and put it on a lower shelf where the biscuits will flop and crack.

Cook for a further 5–10 minutes, then remove from the oven and let them cool on the baking sheet before transferring them to a rack.

SHORTBREAD

In Scotland, shortbread is particularly eaten during the season between Christmas and Hogmanay, when it is always offered to 'first-footers', the first to cross the threshold of the house in the New Year.

MAKES 8 WEDGES

150 g (5 oz) plain flour
60 g (2 oz) rice flour, plus extra for shaping
180 g (6 oz) butter
60 g (2 oz) icing sugar, sifted

*P*reheat the oven to 150°C (300°F, Gas 2).

Put all the ingredients in a bowl and rub in the butter with your fingers until the mixture is like finest breadcrumbs. Then knead the mixture to form a smooth dough with no cracks. Turn it on to a board sprinkled with rice flour and form it into a flat round about 1 cm (½ inch) thick.

Mark the edge all the way round with your fingers and mark into slices or prick with a fork.

Lay the round in a tin lined with buttered greaseproof paper and bake for 45 minutes. Cut it into pieces while it is warm if you like, but allow it to cool in the tin.

BRANDY SNAPS

MAKES ABOUT 35

4 tablespoons golden syrup
125 g (4 oz) butter
125 g (4 oz) plain flour
125 g (4 oz) sugar
1 teaspoon ground ginger
1 teaspoon brandy

*P*reheat the oven to 180°C (350°F, Gas 4).

Heat the syrup in a small saucepan. When it comes to the boil, add the butter and let it melt completely, shaking the pan. Remove the pan from the heat and stir in the remaining ingredients to obtain a thick smooth batter.

Drop teaspoons of the mixture, well-spaced to allow for spreading, on an ungreased baking sheet. Bake for 6–7 minutes to an even golden colour.

Remove the sheet from the oven and allow to cool for about 1 minute. Then remove the brandy snaps 1 at a time with a palette knife, and roll them into cylinders round the handle of a wooden spoon. Work fast because the brandy snaps set quickly and become brittle; if they become too brittle to work, just put the baking sheet back into the warm oven for a couple of minutes.

When cool and crisp, the little cylinders can be filled with whipped cream, flavoured, if you like, with brandy; or they can be eaten as they are.

CHEESE AND OATMEAL BISCUITS

MAKES ABOUT 20

250 g (8 oz) porridge oats or coarse oatmeal
125 g (4 oz) plain flour
60 g (2 oz) grated cheese – Cheddar and Cheshire are suitable
125 g (4 oz) butter
salt
cayenne pepper
1 egg, beaten

*P*reheat the oven to 170°C (325°F, Gas 3).

These biscuits can be made in a food processor. Process the porridge oats for a few seconds to make them finer but with a few larger pieces. Add the flour, cheese, butter, salt and cayenne and process quickly to a fine, crumbly, dryish mixture. Add the well beaten egg and 3–4 tablespoons water to bind the mixture lightly – keep it on the dryish side.

Or, if you are making the biscuits by hand, rub the butter into the flour and oatmeal, add the cheese, salt and cayenne and then stir in the well beaten egg and enough water to bind the mixture as before.

Roll out the dough thinly on a floured board. The dough will be quite crumbly around the edges, but this doesn't matter. Cut into rounds with a 6 cm (2½ inch) pastry cutter or wine glass and space the biscuits out on a buttered baking sheet. Bake for 20–25 minutes or a little longer – they should be crisp all the way through when they are cool, but not browned.

Eat when cool with butter and cream cheese. Celery is rather good with these; use only the tender, pale yellow, inner stalks, and keep the stringy outer stalks for making soup.

CURRIED CHEESE STRAWS

MAKES ABOUT 20

Make half the quantity of Rough Puff Pastry (see right) and, while you are rolling and turning it, sprinkle each layer with a little finely grated Parmesan cheese mixed with curry powder – use 30 g (1 oz) cheese and 1 teaspoon curry powder altogether.

A CONTENTED COUNTRY CAT.

Preheat the oven to 200°C (400°F, Gas 6).

After the final folding, roll out the pastry to .5 cm (¼ inch) thick and cut into strips about 1 cm (½ inch) wide. Twist the strips and put them on a wetted baking sheet, well spread apart. Bake for 8–10 minutes, until crisp, light and brown. These straws burn very suddenly, so take care.

SHORTCRUST PASTRY

For open pies, plate pies, tarts and so forth. Salty, crisp English butter gives the right texture and flavour to the pastry.

MAKES ABOUT 300 G (10 OZ), ENOUGH FOR ONE 24 CM (9½ INCH) FLAN CASE

150 g (5 oz) plain flour
30 g (1 oz) self-raising flour
125 g (4 oz) butter, very cold (or use half butter, half vegetable fat shortening

TO MAKE SHORTCRUST PASTRY

Sieve the 2 flours together in a bowl. Cut the butter into the flour with a knife, holding the butter in 1 hand and carving off thin flakes of butter with the other. Rub the flakes quickly into the flour — stop as soon as the mixture starts to become heavy and clings to your fingers. The texture of coarse large crumbs is right.

Add water — a couple of tablespoons at first and then a little at a time until you can just collect the pastry together into a mass. Form it into a ball, cover and chill at least 1 hour in the refrigerator; remove 20–25 minutes before using.

To use the pastry, flatten it quickly with a rolling pin to loosen it and roll it out on a lightly floured board.

TO MAKE A FLAN CASE

Line a well-buttered flan tin with the pastry, prick the base with a fork and trim the edges, pushing the pastry neatly into the sides of the tin. Fill with crumpled foil and chill, or bake at once.

Allow 12–15 minutes at 190°C (375°F, Gas 5) and then remove the foil and add the filling. If it is to be served cold and will not get any more cooking in the oven, turn down the temperature to 170°C (325°F, Gas 3) and allow a further 10–15 minutes without the foil.

ROUGH PUFF PASTRY

This is a quick alternative to flaky pastry and easy to make. To make other quantities, keep the proportion of flour and fat the same and use the same technique.

MAKES ABOUT 500 G (1 LB)

250 g (8 oz) butter straight from the refrigerator, cubed
250 g (8 oz) plain flour
salt

Sieve the flour and a little salt into a bowl, add the butter and cut it into the flour with a sharp knife until it is in pea-size pieces. Add 1 tablespoon cold water and stir it in with the knife blade, then add 1–2 tablespoons more until you can gather the dough into a ball. Flatten the ball, score it twice with a knife and wrap in foil. Chill for 20 minutes.

Roll the dough out into a rectangle 30×15 cm (12×6 inches) and fold into thirds like a letter. Turn it round 90° and roll and fold again. Use flour to prevent the pastry from sticking but not to much at a time, as it will make the pastry heavy. Chill for 15 minutes.

Repeat the rolling and folding 2 or 3 times more, chilling in between each folding operation. Use whenever a recipe calls for puff or flaky pastry.

CRIMPING THE EDGE OF A PIE

THERE ARE SEVERAL WAYS OF MAKING THE EDGE OF A PIECRUST LOOK PRETTY AND STICK FIRMLY TO THE EDGE OF ITS PIE DISH.

1. THE FIRST IS THE SIMPLE FORK METHOD — USE THE PRONGS OF A FORK TO MAKE A RIDGED PATTERN ALL THE WAY ROUND THE EDGE. KEEP THE FORK AT AN ANGLE TOWARDS THE CENTRE OF THE PIE SO THAT THE CUT EDGE OF THE PASTRY DOES NOT BECOME FLATTENED.

2. SCALLOP THE EDGE BY PRESSING THE RIM WITH YOUR THUMB OR THE HANDLE END OF A SPOON, WHILE MAKING A VERTICAL DENT IN THE CUT EDGE OF THE PASTRY WITH THE BACK OF A KNIFE AT THE SIDE OF EVERY INDENTATION.

3. USING A SMALL, OLD-FASHIONED MEAT SKEWER WITH A ROUND LOOP TOP, PRESS THE TOP INTO THE RIM OF THE PASTRY ALL THE WAY ROUND; KEEP IT AT AN ANGLE TO AVOID FLATTENING THE CUT EDGE OF THE PASTRY. THIS GIVES A PRETTY PATTERN OF CIRCLES, EACH CIRCLE JUST TOUCHING THE NEXT ONE.

4. MAKE A ROPE PATTERN BY TWISTING A PINCH OF THE PASTRY EDGE INWARDS; CONTINUE TO PINCH AND TWIST ALL THE WAY ROUND THE RIM.

INDEX

ACKNOWLEDGEMENTS

The publisher thanks the following photographers and organizations for their kind permission to reproduce the photographs in this book: 11 right Fine Art Photographic Library; 13 Pia Tryde; 17 The Anthony Blake Photo Library; 21 Ianthe Ruthven; 33 Ianthe Ruthven; 35 right Fine Art Photographic Library (courtesy Julian Simon); 38 Jacqui Hurst; 40 Trevor Wood/Image Bank; 41 Jacqui Hurst; 49 right Fine Art Photographic Library (Hampshire Gallery); 53 Ann Kelley; 55 Clay Perry/Arcaid; 62 George Wright; 63 Zefa Picture Library; 65 right Fine Art Photographic Library; 70 Jerry Harpur (Jill Austwick, Hobart); 72 Debbie Patterson; 73 George Wright; 75 Andrew Lawson; 85 right Bridgeman Art Library; 87 IPC Magazines Ltd 1991/Robert Harding Syndication; 93 Glyn Satterley; 96 Andrew Lawson; 99 Michael Busselle; 109 right Fine Art Photographic Library; 110 Lucy Mason; 120 S & O Mathews; 122 Glyn Satterley; 125 right Fine Art Photographic Library; 126 Ianthe Ruthven; 136 S & O Mathews; 137 David Burton Associates; 139 right Fine Art Photographic Library; 148 Ianthe Ruthven; 151 Camera Press/Michelle Garrett; 153 right Fine Art Photographic Library (Burlington Paintings); 154 Jacqui Hurst; 155 Ken Kirkwood/Arcaid; 158 IPC Magazines Ltd 1990/Robert Harding Syndication; 171 right Fine Art Photographic Library (Courtesy of Rafael Valls Fine Paintings); 177 Niall Clutton/Arcaid; 186 La Maison de Marie Claire/Chabaneix/Bayle.

The following photographs were specially taken for Conran Octopus by Peter Williams:

10–11, 12, 15, 19, 23, 26, 29, 30, 34–35, 36, 39, 42–43, 44–45, 47, 48–49, 50–51, 56–57, 59, 60–61, 64–65, 68–69, 76, 79, 80–81, 82, 84–85, 88–89, 94–95, 97, 101, 103, 107, 108–109, 113, 114–115, 116–117, 119, 121, 124–125, 129, 130, 133, 134, 138–139, 140–141, 145, 146–147, 149, 152–153, 157, 160–161, 165, 167, 168–169, 170–171, 173, 174–175, 178–179, 182.

The publisher would also like to thank Eileen MacPhee of the Sea Fish Industry Authority, Edinburgh.

CAROLINE CONRAN'S ACKNOWLEDGEMENTS
If this book does well, much of its success will be due to the wonderful work done by Peter Williams, the photographer; Mary Evans, the art director; Sue Storey, the designer; the contributions of Jane Suthering and Abigail Ahern, and the enthusiasm and tolerance of Anne Furniss and Beverly Le Blanc.

I should also like to say thank you to my friend Susan Campbell, who first gave me the confidence to write a cookery book, and to Linda Merto, Wendy Jones and Philippa Theophinides for helping to make life manageable when I am under pressure.